# THE
# DOLLAR
# FARMER

ISBN Paperback: 979-8-9989262-0-4
ISBN EBook: 979-8-9989262-1-1

*To Sharon, Jacob, and Ariel*
*who inspire me each day to live, laugh, love, learn,*
*and leave the world a better place than I found it.*

# THE DOLLAR $ FARMER

## How the Rich Make Money While They Sleep (And How You Can Too)

JOSE L. MARTIN, CFP®

# Contents

## PART IV. "HARVEST"

# Introduction

"If you couldn't read, how'd you make it all the way to Fire Chief, Louis?" I asked.

Louis, a gentle Key West "Conch" with leathery skin and a heart of gold winked from behind his bespectacled eyes, "I faked it real good, Jose."

He sat across the table from me. Moments later, he'd share words that would change the trajectory of my life and that would ultimately culminate in the writing of this book.

Like many prospects I worked with, Louis and Genie - a couple in their fifties - were referred to me so that I could assist them in their financial and investment planning as they prepared for the years commonly referred to as "retirement". I was relatively young in my career and still learning how to navigate the challenges of working with individuals and couples who wanted to find a successful and secure pathway through retirement. Most were arriving to retirement in the traditional way: find a career, make a living, and save a bit of each paycheck into an investment account with the hopes that one day, it - along with Social Security - would be enough to pay for a retirement lifestyle. And as a young financial advisor, I was gaining expertise in this field.

But Louis and Genie came to me with a unique challenge: Louis – as a result of his dyslexia, was incapable of independently managing their financial affairs. This wouldn't have been a problem as Genie, a highly competent and educated attorney with a successful practice, had always taken care of the household finances. But recently, a tragedy had derailed their plans: Genie had been diagnosed with early onset Alzheimer's Disease and her cognitive ability was deteriorating rapidly. In and of itself, it was devastating news. While we'd be able to help Louis and Genie navigate their financial future with proper planning and by putting the right people and systems in place, what could not be remedied was the impact it would have on their lives in the years to come.

When Louis had an opportunity to speak with me privately, he shared insights that impacted me profoundly. He talked about how hard they had each worked and saved so that they could one day retire and travel the world together. Louis said, "Jose, we were waiting for this. We worked our whole lives for this. We saved so much and for so long. For me to retire and for Genie to sell her practice so that we could enjoy these years together. Our 'Golden Years'. And we thought we'd do everything we had planned for. And now this....We won't be able to do any of it."

Then, he pulled me in close, looked me dead in the eye and said, "Don't wait...whatever it is you want your life to be. Whatever it is you want to do...*Don't wait.*" I'll never forget those words.

I was more than 25 years his junior but the lesson was imprinted on me. Still, I thought to myself as I considered both my life and that of my clientele, "*How can a person achieve the financial ability and flexibility to do what they want when they want?*" I recognized that as a Financial Planner and Investment Advisor, I was building a business that might provide such possibilities. But for most people in traditional careers, how could they achieve financial freedom in a compressed time frame? I had been taught that the singular path to financial independence - the one most people should follow - is the "*save and grow rich slowly over time*". Invest a little from each paycheck and eventually (read:

*after several decades*), you'll *maybe* have enough to leave the workforce.

For the next several years, I continued building a business that counseled clients on how to successfully retire *after* they'd built a sufficient nest-egg while pondering non-traditional pathways to financial independence. I wanted to not only live a life of "don't wait!" as Louis had counseled but also provide to my friends, clients, and loved-ones, the tools to be able to do the same for themselves. To achieve financial freedom at any time and any age.

Then something wholly unexpected occurred that would change the trajectory of my life and shift my paradigm. In 2015, Ariel, my 14 year old daughter started goofing around on a burgeoning social media app called *musical.ly* (the precursor to the now infamous *TikTok* app). She'd make 15 second lip-syncing videos to her favorite songs and share them with her friends. She had a unique talent to creatively move her camera phone in sync to the music while making gestures and facial expressions that were undeniably entertaining.

One Friday morning, a video she created was featured on the app's front page and the rest, as they say, is history. She went from having 50 followers that morning to over 50,000 by the following Monday. Within a week, she had 500,000 followers and soon, millions. As of this writing, she has over 45 million followers across all platforms. At first, my wife and I didn't quite know how to process this new reality. We wondered, "*Who are these people looking at our 14 year old daughter? Is she safe? Is there anything we need to do?*"

But soon, we came to recognize that this new digital world was as viable as traditional movies, TV, and music as a form of entertainment. Social Media and Digital Content were "the new Hollywood" so-to-speak. In making that discovery, we came to learn that there were new revenue opportunities for those willing and able to create and share digital content on places like Instagram and YouTube. And that revenue flowed in recurring fashion. Make one video and get paid for it over and over and over....

My daughter recognized this as an opportunity to launch a career in the entertainment industry. Now, nearly a decade later, she has enjoyed work as a YouTube creator, professional actor, recording artist, and author all the while earning substantial amounts of ongoing, recurring revenue. What I describe as "farmed income" in the book. My daughter was the first Dollar Farmer I knew. Or rather, she was the first example of Dollar Farming I recognized as such. It was her example and this brave new world we'd been thrust into that opened my eyes and answered that gnawing question: *"How can a person achieve the financial ability and flexibility to do what they want when they want?"*

Surely, if my daughter could embark on a path that would create financial freedom and fulfillment at age 14, *then anyone could at any age.* One didn't need to rely on the sole method of "saving and investing" a percentage of their income over a decades-long career. I recognized that her example fit in what the book will describe as the *"Creative"* category of Dollar Farms, i.e., one where a person's intellectual property - their idea - is the seed that creates the income stream. I also understood that not everyone will have the creative spark or energy to make their mark in the way my daughter did nor will they necessarily have the good fortune to suddenly "go viral" on social media as it were.

*Still,* I thought to myself, *there must be other ways that a person can create recurring revenue streams.* If my daughter could do it by creating digital content and I could do it by using the right business structure, aren't there other methods and tactics a person could use? It was then as I allowed my thoughts to expand and think deeply, creatively, and from a new perspective that I started seeing Dollar Farms everywhere. In ATM machines. Print-On-Demand businesses. Franchises. Rental Properties. In fact, all businesses. I felt a deep sense of both fulfillment and purpose.

In my 20+ years in the industry as a Financial Planner and Advisor, I've counseled far too many people who've worked too long and too hard and have still "come up short". I know too many young adults who look at the world before them with fear and apprehension about their financial futures. And I have been around as many wonderful people mired in careers they can't stand but still feel they can't leave for fear of the financial consequences. This book is for all of them. It is not an operations manual - it simply can't be. But it is intended to be a seed of hope planted in the reader's imagination which in turn can germinate and launch a world of financial possibilities.

I don't know how many lives this book will touch or how many people it will help achieve financial freedom and fulfillment. But I am driven by a passion and purpose to do my bit. And because I firmly believe that each one of us makes a direct impact in the history of humanity, then a life lived "on purpose" makes the greatest possible positive impact. If by helping just one person achieve financial freedom so that they can in turn live by such a purpose, then this book will be a success. Your journey to financial freedom starts now. *Don't Wait...*

# PART I

# "Choice"

"If you don't find a way to make money while you sleep, you will work until you die."

—Warren Buffett

### Chapter 1

# Quiet Desperation

*"My life is not my own...."*

The thought struck Casey like thunder rattling her bones. A pang of confusion and guilt quickly followed the thought. After all, here she was with everything she'd ever planned for - everything she ever wanted. She was 28 years old with a solid mid-level marketing position and an MBA. She was engaged to her college sweetheart who had recently landed a gig with a great corporate law firm. She had income security and great benefits.

And yet - something had hit her hard about the conversation with Jordan Steele, the VP of Marketing that she reported to.

"I'm sorry, Casey," he'd told her. "You know that I can't let you take vacation the week of the 9th - I'll need you for the product launch," he said.

She knew he was right. Their new product line-up would be announced the week before Black Friday / Cyber Monday and the 9th was only two weeks before that. It would be "all hands on deck" to prepare for the announcement. The product launches would then follow, with a full-court press through Christmas. In other words, no week off until after the new year. But it wasn't even a vacation she yearned for. It was the ability to get away *that week*.

The week of November 9th was her parents' 40th anniversary cruise - a family reunion that would gather her siblings, aunts & uncles, and cousins from around the country. It would be a once-in-a-lifetime event that would pay tribute to her parents. But it was much more than that. It would also mean missing what would likely be her parents' last anniversary celebration now that her father had been diagnosed with inoperable cancer. The prognosis for him was not good and he had five - maybe six months left following the anniversary cruise. This was not only a celebration but a goodbye of sorts for everyone in the way her father wanted it.

She forced a smile and nodded, "Of course. I understand."

Mr. Steele smiled back, "Great! Now - do you have everything you need for the presentation with Mr. Bloom?"

"I do," she replied. Elijah Bloom was her first "solo" account. He was an affable, middle-aged man whose account she'd taken over when Jordan Steele was promoted to VP a few months back.

"Remember - he's not into spreadsheets and pie charts. Sell him with your charm and personality," Mr. Steele counseled. "Where are you meeting?"

"We're meeting for lunch at his country club."

Mr. Steele chuckled, "Ah yes - he loves to meet after a round of morning golf. Definitely avoid numbers. He won't be in the mood for it."

One thing she'd learned about Elijah Bloom was that he enjoyed meeting in settings that seemed distinctly "non-business" related. When accompanying Mr. Steele over several months as he prepared her for the hand-off of some of his accounts, they had met Elijah at a wine-tasting, a japanese garden, and at a boatyard. The first time she'd met him was at a boutique art gallery. Never once had they met in an office or conference room. And she always admired how jovial - how sunny Mr. Bloom was.

As she walked away from her boss' office, she had a moment when the thought of Elijah's warm disposition lifted her spirits. But as she reached her desk and gathered the presentation materials for their meeting, she'd already slipped back into a morose state as she realized she'd miss her parents' anniversary and that last opportunity to gather with her entire family before it was too late. All because she couldn't take a week off work when she'd need it.

*"My life is not my own..."*


TRAFFIC WAS ESPECIALLY BRUTAL on her way to the lunch meeting. Casey had always given herself a 20 minute buffer but today, she could have used 40 minutes. Between the traffic, her disappointment at missing the anniversary cruise, and her regular pre-presentation adrenaline, Casey arrived at the meeting less than composed.

She walked through the country club's restaurant onto its patio seating area that overlooked the lush island green of the 18th hole. A whiff of sweet magnolia caught her as she hustled toward Elijah's table. He sat with his back facing the restaurant, taking in the beautiful view.

She took a deep breath, then said, "I'm so sorry to be late, Mr. Bloom." As he turned slowly, she expected the disappointment that most top executives convey when they perceive their time has been disrespected. Instead, Elijah greeted her with a sunny smile and a gentle nod.

"Don't be silly, Casey," he said. "Look at this beautiful view on this splendid day I've been able to enjoy. And please - call me Elijah."

She smiled. *"Is he for real?"* she wondered.

"What's wrong, Casey?" he asked. She realized that the short respite of his warm greeting must have been betrayed by her underlying anxiety. Now, she felt especially frustrated that she'd brought that energy to an important business meeting.

"It's nothing Mr. Bloom," she shook her head.

He cleared his throat and raised a brow.

"I'm sorry," she blushed, "Elijah."

He nodded, "That's better."

Casey looked down, now wondering if she'd even be able to go forward with the marketing presentation she'd prepared. She started, "Thank you for the opportunity to meet, Elijah. I'd like to share some exciting new opportunities within our product portfolio that you might find interesting...." She trailed off, realizing that she was giving what was an obviously canned pitch. And moreso, she could tell that Mr. Bloom could see right through it. She put her head down, now fully embarrassed.

"Look Casey," Elijah started, "I don't know if there's something going on - something that is making you feel uncomfortable. But I don't want you to stress about it - certainly not with me and especially not over a presentation." She appreciated his generosity and nodded. He continued, "If you have anything you want to share, I'm happy to listen. But above all, if there's something you're working through, I especially don't want you to feel any pressure about making a sales pitch today. You've already earned my trust and confidence. Business will take care of itself in time."

He motioned towards the view, "We can sit, enjoy a nice lunch with the beautiful view, and talk about anything we feel like. Or not talk at all - that's fine too."

It was as if a thousand pound weight had been lifted from her shoulders. She smiled in deep appreciation, took a seat, and inhaled deeply to absorb the beautiful, pungent scent of sweet magnolias wafting through the breeze.

CASEY HADN'T MEANT TO spill her guts and share her sorrows to Elijah Bloom. But after his kindness and compassion, the floodgates opened and Casey let it all out. She shared her sadness about not being able to take the week off and missing the family's anniversary cruise. And mostly, about the future remorse and guilt she knew she was going to feel when it was all said and done.

"I'm sorry. I didn't mean to lay that all on you," she said as she looked down at her feet, like a child who'd just realized they'd admitted more than they should to the Assistant Principal.

"Don't apologize. I value authenticity and sincerity far more than business or money," he answered. "And I appreciate that you feel comfortable enough with me to share your feelings. Friends are hard to come by so I hope I can be one for you," he said.

She blushed a bit then smiled.

"What you shared makes my heart ache. I can only imagine how difficult it must be for you to feel that you have to choose between your career ambitions and the opportunity to spend this invaluable time with your family," he said.

She nodded as the frustration roared within her.

"And I hate to tell you that life, if you remain on this path, will continue to pelt you with these types of choices until you acquiesce and feel it is no choice at all," Elijah expressed.

Casey shook her head, "It's so frustrating."

Elijah looked down, then back at Casey. He hesitated a moment, clearly drawn with a tinge of apprehension before speaking, "This may be out of line so don't be shy to tell me so. But can I offer you a bit of unsolicited guidance?"

Casey nodded, "Yes, please. I appreciate all the good guidance I can get."

Elijah smiled compassionately, "If you don't want your life to be filled with these kinds of regrets and 'no-win' scenarios, you're gonna have to make a choice," Elijah remarked.

"What choice?" Casey asked.

"About what you want your life to be like," he answered, "and about whether your life is to be your own."

She shook her head slowly. "But I still don't understand. How do I make that choice?"

He continued, "Before I answer, let me ask you a question: What's your most valuable asset?"

She thought for a moment, then shrugged her shoulders. "I suppose my house is…even though the bank owns most of it," she laughed.

He smiled, "Most people would probably answer the same. Some might say, 'my retirement account' or, 'my investments'. But invariably, most people look at something that they've assigned a monetary value to and point to it as their most valuable asset."

She looked puzzled. "Is that wrong?"

Elijah nodded, "It is." He continued, "A few people may answer something along the lines of, 'my ability to earn income is my most valuable asset'."

She sat back and pondered that for a moment. Something swirled in her as she replied, "Yeah, I suppose that's true. None of those other things are even possible if I can't make a living. If I can't work, then I can't pay my mortgage or put money away for retirement."

"Good. You're starting to see the forest," he replied. "But

there's something far more valuable - far more precious than even your ability to earn a living."

She searched her mind for the answer he was looking for but nothing came.

Elijah leaned in, "What's the one thing you can never get back?"

*Of course*, she thought. "My time. Time is the one thing I can never get back," she nodded. "So *time* is my most valuable asset?"

"Right. Time is so valuable that it is in fact *invaluable*. Now you have to ask yourself, 'Am I willing to trade my most valuable asset for money?'" he continued.

"I'm not sure I follow," Casey said.

Elijah replied, "Earlier, I'd told you that you'd have to make a choice. The choice is whether you'll continue to trade your time for dollars. It's the most important financial decision you'll ever make."

"But if I stop working, I won't get paid. I'd go broke," Casey countered.

"Hmm," Elijah started, "So you equate the hours you work with how you get paid?"

"Of course," Casey answered. "Well, maybe not by the hour but in general, yes. How else would I earn money?"

Elijah drew a slow, deep breath. He looked carefully at Casey before responding, "Am I working right now?"

She shrugged her shoulders, "Not sure how to answer. I guess technically, sort of. This was setup as a business meeting." Casey looked down sheepishly, "Even though I derailed it. But technically, it's a business meeting so I think, yeah, you're working."

He chuckled. "Let me rephrase it then. The four hours before you arrived, while I was out golfing with an old friend, was I working then?"

"I guess not," she said.

"But during those hours, would you believe, I was still generating income? Doesn't that contradict what you just said?"

"Well, in a way, I guess it does. But I still don't understand. I mean, how can I stop working and still get paid?" Casey asked.

"You'll need to start *farming* your dollars rather than *gathering* or *hunting* them," Elijah answered.

She looked puzzled.

"If you want your life to truly be your own, you'll need to become a *Dollar Farmer*."

"I APOLOGIZE IF I appear a bit cynical," Casey remarked, "but, a *Dollar Farmer*? Are you serious?" she asked, searching his face for a hint of sarcasm or humor. "What's the old expression: 'Money doesn't grow on trees'?"

He smiled, "Of course it doesn't." He drew a long sip of his coffee. "Or does it?" He chuckled as he shrugged his shoulders.

She laughed, "Ok, I'll play along. Tell me more."

"Remember the 'choice' I mentioned earlier?" Elijah asked. "About trading your hours for dollars?"

She nodded.

"What if you didn't have to do that? What if you could wake up on January 1st knowing you'd have enough money coming in to enjoy your desired lifestyle for the whole year without having to go to work?" Elijah asked. "What if you could choose to do with your time as you wished without money being a concern? How would you feel?"

Again, Casey studied Elijah's expression for a betrayal in his otherwise earnest tone. There was none.

After a beat, she replied, "Who wouldn't want that? I mean, what you're describing sounds like everybody's wish. Like winning the lottery. Or retiring."

"You're right," he answered, "it's the reason most people buy lottery tickets. Because they're hoping they'll be able to suddenly and quickly have enough money to never have to work again. It's also the reason most people spend most of their adult lives working with the hope that one day, they'll be able to *'retire'*. To stop *'working for money'*."

Casey looked down, a feeling of sadness washing over her.

"What's wrong?" he asked.

A tear came to her eye. She explained, "What you just said, about a person working their whole life to one day be able to retire...it made me think of my Dad. He worked 40 years at the same company, putting money away so that he and my Mom could enjoy retirement together." She swallowed hard and took a slow, deep breath. "He retired two years ago. And now he's got less than a year to live and...." her voice trailed off.

Elijah shook his head mournfully. "I'm very sorry for what you and your family are going through. It breaks my heart because everything you've said about your father suggests he is a wonderful, loving man."

She nodded.

"I want to be very clear, Casey," he continued, "what I'm suggesting is not at all like winning the lottery. Becoming a *Dollar Farmer* will not mean overnight riches. In fact, it will require an extraordinary amount of patience, tenacity, and yes - hard, hard work. Very hard work."

Casey looked at Elijah with an appreciation for his compassion and candor.

He said, "And the last thing I'd want to do is trivialize the value of work - especially the hard work done by good people like your father."

She smiled.

"Becoming a *Dollar Farmer* is first and foremost a change in mindset. *A shift in how you view your relationship between work and income,*" he counseled. "But making that shift, and then taking the right actions over time will allow you to unlink your time from your income. It means you'll achieve what I described earlier: control over how you choose to spend your time. Or more succinctly: how you gain *financial freedom and fulfillment.*"

She sat back and asked, "But isn't that what 'saving for retirement' is? By putting money away in my retirement account?"

"Sure," he answered, "that's one way of doing it. The old school, very traditional way. And it is in fact, a form of dollar farming. There's nothing wrong with that. And you can do that if you're okay with taking decades to get there. In the meantime, you'd be spending years of your life making the financial trade of hours for dollars. And you won't have the freedom to make choices about how you spend the days in your life along the way."

"There's a different way?" she asked.

He nodded. "I'd be happy to show you," he answered, "but I'd need you to understand two very important things that I've already alluded to: first, being a *Dollar Farmer* is not a get-rich-quick overnight scheme. Like I said earlier, it will take patience, hard work, and tenacity."

"Ok," she replied, "and what's the second thing?"

He continued, "That I'm not making a value judgment on people like your father who have chosen the lifetime career path. Work is honorable. Work truly is a virtue and I believe we all have an obligation to society to be productive, contributing members."

Casey listened intently.

He said, "In fact, though you see me enjoy my time - here at a golf course, or a few weeks back when we met at an art gallery - I happily spend countless hours contributing energy and effort to causes and organizations I care about. One should always find ways to work and be productive. The key is in not having 'how much' you work or 'when' you work determine your income."

"I also want to emphasize that I am not suggesting that you'll suddenly be able to live a life that is free from 'work'," he said. "Rather, what I want to impress upon you is that we are examining the idea of how you are compensated for your work. And more importantly, how you gain freedom and ownership over your most valuable asset: your time."

"So you're saying that by becoming a," she paused as she searched for the term, "*Dollar Farmer*, I'd be able to make money and also do what I want when I want? Like take a cruise with my family whenever I feel like it?"

Elijah chuckled, "That's oversimplifying it a bit but yes, once you've created successful *Dollar Farms*, you'll be able to enjoy your time as you choose and live with financial security and abundance."

She smiled cautiously. "I don't intend to sound disrespectful, Elijah," she started, "but this sounds a bit far-fetched. A little too good to be true."

"I understand," he answered. "But I assure you *Dollar Farming* is real and not a scheme. I can teach you how to regain control of your life and time if you're willing to learn. You can achieve what I'd describe as *financial freedom*."

"When you say financial freedom," she asked, "do you mean being wealthy? Rich?"

"I'm glad you asked. In fact, maybe it's important that we define our terms carefully. Let's start with that term: financial freedom," Elijah said. "Most people who save a bit of each paycheck into a retirement plan like a 401(k) are doing so because they hope to be able to retire someday, wouldn't you agree?"

Casey nodded.

"Ultimately, they hope to have sufficient savings and investments to generate enough monthly income that, along with other sources of income like Social Security and Pension checks, they'll be able to enjoy their lives without having to 'work' anymore," he explained. "We use the term 'retirement' to describe what it is these people are striving towards because they *retire from work*. It's a descriptor for their relationship to their former career. But if we're modifying our terms to reflect their *state of being* and instead describe what they've accomplished rather than their relationship to their former career, I would use the term, 'financial freedom' because now, they have enough income to live whether they 'choose' to work or not. They are in fact 'free' from a financial standpoint."

"Wow," Casey reflected. "I would have never looked at it that way."

Elijah smiled, "That's understandable - our society doesn't really help orient our thinking towards our relationship to money or work in a way that makes *Dollar Farming* and *Financial Freedom* logical. But what a retiree has done by saving a bit of their income into a retirement plan over a 30 year work cycle is create a *Dollar Farm*. And their objective over that time wasn't to 'retire' per se but rather, to achieve *Financial Freedom*. The difference is that what I'm trying to help guide you towards are solutions - Dollar Farms - that can help get you there much, much faster than over 30 years. But I emphasize: it won't be easy and it won't happen overnight."

"Aren't I too old to start this? I'm already almost 30," Casey asked.

Elijah laughed at her innocence and naivete. "I'm sorry, Casey

- I mean no disrespect. But no - not only are you not too old - you are young enough that it will allow you to enjoy decades of your life with the freedom to use your time how you choose to. But to take your question a step further, I have counseled many people who were already past 60 years old on how to achieve financial freedom and fulfillment as 'Dollar Farmers'. *These lessons can be applied by anyone at any age so long as they're willing to shift their mindset and take the right actions.*"

She sat back and pondered that for a moment. Then she asked, "will I be able to go on my family trip?" she asked.

He chuckled, "That'll be up to you. But in the long run, yes - for the rest of your life, you'll be able to decide what you do with your time and when you do it."

"Then I'm in," Casey answered emphatically.

## Chapter 2

# Hunters & Gatherers

The following week, Casey met Elijah for lunch at a local restaurant. "Ready to become a Dollar Farmer?" Elijah asked.

"Sure," Casey answered, "but what about all the stuff you had me do?" Prior to the meeting, Elijah had asked Casey to complete a scavenger-hunt style list of items. They'd included ordering a children's book from Amazon, going to a specific gas-station and going through its car-wash, bringing a copy of her retirement account statement, and withdrawing cash from an ATM. She also had to compile a list of 1 and 2 bedroom apartment units available for rent in a specific zip code. She felt a bit like the *Karate Kid* who'd had to complete a bunch of random tasks that seemed to have nothing to do with Karate. She hoped these random tasks - like the Karate Kid's lessons - would also somehow circle back to insights from Elijah.

"Ah, yes," he laughed. "We'll get to that soon enough. But first - an introduction to *Dollar Farming*."

She smiled, eager to learn how she might find a way to go on her parents' anniversary cruise.

"Before discussing money or income, let's spend a moment on anthropology," Elijah said.

"Anthropology?" Casey laughed. "Wow - it's like I'm back in college!"

Elijah laughed too. "I think it's important to draw this analogy. It will make the concept of *Dollar Farming* very clear." He sipped his iced tea slowly before continuing, "If we go back to the history of mankind - some 15 or 20 thousand years ago, you'll find that our ancestors spent most of their time concerned with one thing: survival. This meant constantly seeking shelter and food."

Casey listened.

"At the time, early humans traveled in small, nomadic groups following herds of animals they could hunt for food while foraging and gathering edible plants, fruits, and nuts. Once the animal herds migrated or the local vegetation was depleted, they'd move on." Elijah sipped from his glass and continued, "And such was life - a constant churning cycle of hunting, gathering, and traveling. Life didn't allow for many other activities - at least not that we know of."

Casey wondered - *hoped* - that this lesson would somehow bring her closer to understanding how she might attain "financial freedom" as Elijah described it. But she trusted her mentor and he continued the explanation.

"So imagine the awe when one of our ancestors pondered the possibility of farming. The possibility of planting and harvesting crops of edible vegetation. The possibility of domesticating animals - livestock that could readily provide reliable meat, eggs, and milk. What would that mean to the prospects of survival? And what would it mean to how we as a human species could spend our time?"

Casey pondered it a moment before nodding as the revelation

dawned on her, "A predictable source of food - milk and eggs along with fruits, grains, and vegetables meant much more time and energy were available to do other things. It meant not having to constantly travel in search of new sources of food."

"That's right," Elijah remarked, "Knowing that food would be readily available without having to spend most of their time hunting and gathering, it also meant that larger groups of people could co-exist. What had been the work of small, nomadic groups now could accommodate larger populations. Villages and tribes were born. From these, people could specialize in different ways to support their communities. Some could make clothes. Others would specialize in woodworking and later, in iron and steel. People were coming together knowing that there'd be abundant resources to feed them."

Casey smiled, "And it was no longer solely a quest for basic survival - time could be enjoyed doing things that were more meaningful."

Elijah nodded, "That's right."

Then, Casey sat back and wondered, "But Elijah - I'm not sure I'm following the analogy. How does this translate to 'financial freedom'?"

"Ahh, I'm glad you asked," he smiled. "Tell me, Casey, what was the relationship between how much food a person gathered and how much was available to eat?"

Casey thought about it a moment. "Do you mean for the farmers? Or the hunters and gatherers?"

"For the hunters and gatherers," Elijah answered.

"Is this a trick question? There's a direct relationship. The amount gathered was the amount available. Once that food was finished, they had to go hunt or gather more."

Elijah nodded, "That's right. It's a one-to-one correlation. How much is gathered is how much is eaten. Or to perhaps oversimplify it, one shift of work equals one ration of food. One-to-one."

Elijah studied Casey's expression carefully and noticed the subtle shift in her face as if a recognition had started to find its way to her conscious mind. She said, "But with farming, once the crops are planted and harvested, they generate food over and over again. One shift of work equals food that recurs."

"Exactly! The farmer doesn't have to plant the same apple tree over and over. And the apple tree itself doesn't provide a mere single fruit. It provides multitudes each and every season," Elijah added. "The work done by the farmer provides rewards that are leveraged."

"That makes sense. But how does it translate to money and income?" Casey asked.

"Tell me how you earn income, Casey," Elijah prodded.

"I'm paid an annual salary by my company. We also receive a performance bonus if the company does well and meets certain goals," Casey replied.

"So in other words," Elijah countered, "You are paid a one-time salary for one year's work."

"I suppose," Casey replied, "plus the bonus."

"Let's set the bonus aside for a moment. With regards to your salary, if you show up and 'do your job' for that year, is there any wiggle room as to how much you'll be paid?"

Casey shook her head, "Not really."

"And next year, could you take the year off and still be paid again for the work you did this year?" Elijah asked.

She laughed, "That would be the day! Of course not. I have to go out and earn it again."

"So what does that sound like? Looking at the hunting & gathering versus farming example we just gave?" Elijah queried.

She shook her head still trying hard to wrap her head around the analogy.

"I know - I'm asking you to think about income in the same way we thought about how we collected the food we ate. It's difficult," he acknowledged. "Let's try it this way: what was your first job ever?"

She smiled remembering her first teenage job somewhat fondly, "I was the cashier at our local supermarket."

"And how did you get paid for that work?" he asked.

"By the hour. It wasn't much back then - probably $7 an hour," she said.

"So if you worked 10 hours a week, how much would you get paid?" Elijah continued.

Casey computed the simple math equation, "Not taking taxes or deductions into account, $70 for 10 hours."

"Right. 10 hours multiplied by $7 each hour equals $70. If one week, you worked fewer hours, would you still get paid $70?" he queried.

"Of course not - I got paid for the hours I worked," she said.

He continued, "And if you decided to take a whole week off, would you get paid at all?"

She gave him a smirk, "You don't really need me to answer that, do you?"

He laughed, "Touché. So you'd go to work and get paid by the hour. Not any more or any less - just what you worked. *What you gathered.* You were - and still are - a dollar gatherer."

"When you put it that way, it almost sounds like an insult," she answered.

"No offense intended at all. In fact, you do wonderful work and you should be proud of your efforts. It's just that from an income generating standpoint, you'll not be able to leverage your work," he answered.

"I never thought of it that way but I do suppose it's a bit like gathering. One year of work equals one year's salary," she answered.

He nodded, "That's right. It is exactly like gathering and foraging for food. And the bonus you receive at the end of the year is simply a bit extra that you receive because you and your fellow 'gatherers' were able to work together and generate a little extra."

"Ok," she remarked, "I can appreciate the analogy. In a nutshell, you're saying I get paid once for the work I do much like our ancestors only collected one ration of food each time they went out."

"Yep," he said, "that's why I'd refer to you as a 'dollar gatherer'."

"Is there a similar analogy for hunters? Are there 'dollar hunters'?" she asked.

He appreciated her curiosity. "In some regards, I believe there are," he said. "I liken the hunting analogy to commissioned salespeople and to people who are paid *per transaction*. Salespeople who earn commissions stand an even less reliable chance of 'having food' to eat. Unlike dollar gatherers - those who work for hourly wages or salaries - dollar hunters take a higher risk / higher reward outlook towards their income."

"Is that bad?" she asked.

"It's not bad or good - I'm not making a value judgment. It's just a reality. A commissioned salesperson can theoretically work an entire week - 40 full hours of work - and not make a single sale. And if they are a purely commissioned salesperson, they will have worked all that time and have no income to show for it - no food to bring home, so-to-speak," Elijah said.

"Why would anyone ever do that?" she wondered.

"Because the reverse is also true," he explained. "A salesperson is essentially 'betting on themselves'. They believe - often correctly - that their efforts will produce greater results than those of the salaried employees. As a result, they have an opportunity to bring even more 'food' home than if they were just paid by the hour." Elijah continued, "And in some regards, they are buoyed by the intrinsic notion that they are more justly rewarded. After all, they surmise, if they work harder, they get paid more and if they take it easy, they might get paid less. They sometimes look over at the salaried or hourly employees with a bit of contempt since an hourly employee will get paid the same - whether they work hard or not at all."

She nodded, "I can relate to that. There are plenty of people in my office that spend half the day scrolling through social media while I'm busting my ass. But we're paid the same. That part isn't fair."

"It may not feel fair but it's the way the machine is built. And you - I hate to tell you this - are merely a cog in that machine. While you are being paid for your efforts - dollar gathering - the work you do is actually farmer's work. Except you're not farming for yourself - *you're providing the labor for the dollar farm that is your company*," he said without a hint of irony or condescension.

She sat back, now a bit mystified by the direction their conversation had taken. "I'm farming for someone else? Now you're really losing me."

"That's a conversation for another day - and we will have that conversation since it will be vital for you to understand the role of labor on a highly efficient and productive dollar farm," Elijah said. "But for now, we will focus on *your* efforts - *the relationship you have between work and income*."

Casey surmised, "So let me see if I'm understanding correctly: *Dollar Gathering* is any income that is paid in exchange for time worked - such as an hourly wage earner or a salaried employee," she said.

He nodded.

"And *Dollar Hunting* represents income that commissioned salespeople get," she continued.

"Sort of," Elijah interrupted, "I use the term 'commissioned salespeople' but there are a gazillion professions who I think of as Dollar Hunters that probably won't conjure your image of a salesperson. Remember: I also said Dollar Hunters are people who get paid per transaction."

"So not just 'Used Car Salespeople'?" Casey quipped.

"Not at all," he agreed, "How about a CPA?" Elijah asked? "Or an Estate Planning Attorney? Would you think of them as commissioned salespeople?"

Casey sat back and looked at her mentor with an air of bewilderment. "Not at all. I don't think of my accountant or attorneys as 'salespeople' earning a commission."

"And that's where the value judgment part probably threw you. We often reflexively think there's something 'immoral' or even 'slimy' about the idea of 'commissions' or 'salespeople'. That they are deceptively trying to get people to part with their money for their own self-serving reasons. But those are just values we've ascribed over the years. The reality is that in some regards, anyone who gets paid for completing a transaction is in some ways earning a 'commission' for their role as a 'salesperson', aren't they?"

"What do you mean?" she asked. "I pay my CPA to prepare my taxes - they aren't earning a commission for selling something. And our attorney - we paid him to create our legal documents. How are they commissioned salespeople?"

Elijah explained, "Let's see - our friends at the Merriam-Webster dictionary define 'commission' as 'a fee paid to an agent or employee for transacting a piece of business or performing a service'[1]." He went on, "And 'salesperson' is defined as 'a person whose job is to sell a product or service in a given territory, in a store, or by telephone'[2]."

She looked at him, trying to connect the dots of the logic he had posed.

He saw she still wasn't sure about his argument and said, "Your question - 'how are they commissioned salespeople' implies that there's something wrong with what they've done. But your CPA essentially 'sold' you a service - the service of preparing your tax returns for which he earned a fee; a commission. *And there's nothing wrong with that.*"

"Interesting," she exhaled. "And how does that make them Dollar Hunters?"

"Good question. Let's assume that your CPA goes out to market his business all week. He buys ads on the internet and goes to Chamber of Commerce meetings - all trying to drum up business," Elijah said. "How much do you suppose he gets paid to go to those meetings?"

"I'm not sure," she answered.

"I'll help you out. Most independent CPAs or transactional attorneys - just like the car salespeople you referred to earlier - don't get paid until they get someone to pay for the service they provide. Just like a 'hunter' doesn't get to eat until they've bagged a kill. In fact, a very popular expression among salespeople is, 'You eat what you kill'."

She smiled and shook her head in a bit of disbelief, "Dollar

---

1 https://www.merriam-webster.com/dictionary/commission

2 https://www.merriam-webster.com/dictionary/salesperson

Hunters. And if they don't prepare a tax return or prepare a legal document, they don't get paid. They don't eat."

"As I'd mentioned," Elijah said, "there's nothing wrong with being a hunter or a gatherer. Except - it will be very difficult for a dollar hunter or gatherer to ever have the one thing you crave: financial freedom."

She nodded, "Because you can only 'eat' what you've hunted or gathered. You're paid singularly for your work."

He smiled and nodded.

"Tell me more about Dollar Farming," she grinned.

Chapter 3

# The Apple Tree

"When an apple farmer plants his tree, what's his objective?" Elijah asked.

"Obviously, to grow a tree that will bear fruit. That will give apples," she answered.

"And how does that tree supply those apples?" he queried.

"Regularly with each harvest. I suppose dozens - maybe even hundreds - of apples each year," she said. Casey continued, "So farming allows you to receive food over and over for having planted the tree just once. So how do you continue this analogy with income? How would I get paid over and over for a single effort?"

Elijah smiled, "Let's take a look at those assignments I gave you, starting with the book I asked you to order online. How much did you pay for that book?"

Casey thought back to the laundry list of tasks Elijah had asked her to complete prior to their meeting. One of those tasks was ordering a book from Amazon. "It was about $13 I think," Casey answered.

"For her efforts, the author was paid about $5 of that total," he said.

"I can't even go through a drive-thru for $5!" she laughed.

"You're right. But you are only one of about 1000 people who purchased that book this month," he added. "And she has another 4 books that each sell about as many copies."

Casey did some quick math. "So $5 per book multiplied by 1000 books is $5000 per month. Multiply that by an additional 4 books that each sell as much. That comes to more than $25,000 of income each month."

Elijah nodded, "That's right. Now does she have to keep writing those 5 books each and every month?"

Casey replied, "Of course not. She did the work once and gets paid over and over again."

"Even as she plays a round of golf or takes a wine tour of Napa Valley or volunteers at her local food bank," Elijah said.

"Or goes on a family cruise to celebrate her parents' anniversary," Casey finished. She then looked up at Elijah, "But I'm not an author. I don't have any books to sell."

"That's true. Maybe you'll become an author. Or maybe not. This is just one example of Dollar Farming. Let's look at another example. How clean is your car?"

She smiled, "Pretty clean after I ran it through the wash."

"Good! And how much did you pay for that wash?" Elijah asked.

"About $10," Casey replied.

"Ok great. Now, to be clear, the car wash operator has expenses they must account for. Water, soap, supplies, etc. Those costs per wash are about $4.50 which means the owner of the car wash nets a bit more than $5 each time a car goes through. On average, that wash services about 30 cars per day which ends up at 900 cars a month or so. That translates to about $4500 of monthly income from a single car wash. Did the car wash owner need to stand there and manually wash 30 cars each day?"

"Of course not," she answered.

"That's right. He made a capital investment in a car wash and now it pays him each time a car is washed," Elijah said.

Casey sat back and let the words sink in. She was starting to understand Elijah's examples but was still having a difficult time seeing herself within the examples. She looked down at some of the other homework assignments he'd given her.

"Ok," she started, "the apartment rentals you asked me to track. Let me see if I'm understanding this one: a person buys a condominium unit, then rents it out for monthly income. As long as they make more than their mortgage, insurance, and maintenance costs, they earn a profit."

Elijah nodded, "It's starting to make sense, isn't it?"

Casey agreed, "Yes - but help me understand your other example - where I withdrew cash from the ATM."

"That one is deceptively simple. When you withdrew the funds, did it ask if you agreed to pay a service fee?" he asked.

"Yes, I think it was about $4," Casey answered.

"On a simplified level, the owner of the cash machine uses those $4 to pay 'rent' to the location where the ATM is and pay another fee for the network and service provider that links your bank information to the machine which allows the withdrawal. After those expenses are paid, the ATM owner nets the remaining amount - about $2 as profit," he explained. "Averaging 50 transactions per day, the owner collects about $100 daily from a single machine. Imagine that he has 10 machines strategically stationed around town. That would generate $30,000 of monthly income."

"And the ATM owner doesn't need to stand around handing out the cash. It happens automatically," Casey acknowledged.

"That's right," Elijah added, "even as the ATM owner sleeps."

"And what about this?" Casey asked as she handed Elijah a copy of her retirement account statement.

"Like we'd talked about earlier, this is old-school Dollar Farming - and still one of the best ways to farm," he replied. "Putting dollars to work by purchasing investment assets that have an opportunity to grow and generate dividend and interest income is one of the most tried and true ways to grow wealth. It's what we've taught people to do over the last hundred years to save for retirement."

"But you said I shouldn't save money for 'retirement', didn't you?" Casey asked.

Elijah held up a finger, "I never said that. In fact, I invest consistently each month in a stock portfolio - it is one of the foundational pieces of my Dollar Farms."

He realized she wasn't quite following his line of thinking and continued, "What I did want to point out is that the traditional path to 'retirement' which consists of setting aside a small amount of money from each paycheck into an investment portfolio is normally a slow, slow way to achieve financial freedom. And that it would take most people decades to hopefully one day get there if it is the only thing they do."

"What about the FIRE movement? Doesn't that help people achieve financial freedom at a young age?" she asked.

Elijah sat back, "Ah, the FIRE movement - *Financial Independence / Retire Early*. The FIRE movement espouses a philosophy that can be effective. It suggests that a person lives at essentially a bare, subsistence level and invest most of their earnings. In other words, if you earned $50,000 a year after taxes, you'd have to live on $15,000 and save $35,000. Welcome to the world of never going out to dinner or taking a vacation. Never enjoying a glass of wine or a round of golf. Living in accommodations far smaller without any creature comforts - all so that you can hopefully save the money within 10 years that you'd need to live on for the next 60. Let's just say, I'm not a fan of this approach."

"Yeah, I guess though it could work, it wouldn't be much fun getting there," Casey responded.

"Not only that," Elijah added, "there are people who have been able to effectively save lots of money by living a subsistence lifestyle and achieve their financial objective. But it has come with a cost: their emotional well-being. Along the way, the stress of living so frugally both damages the journey towards financial independence as well as making it difficult to suddenly retire afterwards and enjoy the fruits of that labor. Most people can't so suddenly transition from living in subsistence mode for a decade to enjoying the opportunities that abundance provides."

"And there are other ways to get there. To achieve financial freedom by being a Dollar Farmer," she added.

"Exactly. So let's define 'Dollar Farming'. With everything we've discussed, tell me in your words what 'Dollar Farming' means to you," he said.

Casey thought about it for a moment. "Well, if 'Dollar Gathering' represents income that employees earn working hourly or salaried positions, that is, trading 'time for money' - and 'Dollar Hunting' means income that is earned as commissions or as a result of the completion of a transaction," she said, pausing to reflect, *"then 'Dollar Farming' is income that is paid over and over for work that was done once."*

He smiled then added, "Very good. In fact, you added a word that I'd wanted to introduce to the conversation - one that helps highlight the essential difference between 'Farmed Dollars' versus those dollars which are 'Hunted' or 'Gathered'. You used the word 'earned' when describing both 'Dollar Gathering' and 'Dollar

Hunting'. That is a critically astute observation."

Casey blushed, "To be fair, Elijah, I hadn't consciously realized I even used the word."

"That's okay," he added, "but it shows that on a deeper level you're starting to understand the important distinction - one that I'd wanted to bring to light throughout our work together. That distinction is that often, people who study or discuss forms of income divide them into two separate categories: 'earned' and 'unearned'. Another set of terms you might hear which mirror these are 'active' and 'passive'. In fact, even the IRS uses such terms as it categorizes the types of taxes that are paid on different types of income."

Casey sat up, "So 'Dollar Hunting' and 'Dollar Gathering' would be considered 'earned' or 'active' income!"

"That's right! And why are they called that, do you suppose?" Elijah pressed.

"Because to receive income from 'Hunted' or 'Gathered' activities, the person needs to 'earn' it 'actively'. They have to 'work' for it to generate the income. And if they don't 'work' or 'actively earn' it, then no income is generated," she concluded.

"Bingo. It's like we said earlier: one shift of work equals one ration of income."

"You showed me a bunch of different ways to farm for dollars - gosh it sounds so hokey just saying it! But honestly, I don't know what to do. I wouldn't even know where to start," she confessed.

"I understand. I wouldn't expect you to," he answered compassionately. "There is no singular method that will work for everyone. And the examples I gave you are simply that - examples. There are countless others and you will be limited only by your creativity and willingness to apply yourself. But I'm happy to help illuminate the way forward if you are interested in learning," he said.

She smiled back, "I'm ready to learn. I want to be a Dollar Farmer. What happens next?"

"There are six steps you'll need to learn with each one building on the previous one. Each step is important and none should be skipped," he told her.

"What are the six steps?" she asked.

"I call them the 'Six F's'," Elijah replied.

"Six F's?" Casey laughed. "That's very clever marketing!"

Elijah laughed too, "That's high praise coming from a marketing expert!" He said, "Yes, I find that by using simple tools like acronyms and alliteration, it makes it easier to remember and apply useful information. So each of the steps we're going to cover is named after a word that starts with the letter 'F'."

"Very cool," Casey remarked, "So let me guess, one of the words is 'Farm' as in 'Farmer'!"

He nodded, "You're going to be a quick study, I see. Yes, 'Farm' is one of the words but it isn't the first word we'll learn. Actually, it's the fourth."

"Wow," she said, "so there are three steps to becoming a Dollar Farmer ahead of 'Farming' itself, huh? What's the first step?"

"Are you ready to get your hands dirty?" Elijah asked.

**TO DO | Make a list of every job or career you've ever had and how you were compensated for it. Then, write down whether you were a Dollar Gatherer, Hunter, or Farmer in each of those roles. Lastly, make note of what you liked and disliked about each job.**

# PART II

# "Arrange"

"There are dreamers, and there are planners; the planners make their dreams come true."

—Edwin Louis Cole

## Chapter 4

# Digging In The Dirt

*"Get my hands dirty?"* Casey hadn't understood what Elijah meant by the comment. But after 3 hours of sorting salvaged food items at a local soup kitchen followed by another 3 hours of working the food line, her hands were both dirty and exhausted.

After the shift, she and Elijah sat outside on a park bench.

"How was that for you?" Elijah asked.

"Tiring....and very rewarding," Casey answered.

He nodded, "Yes, it can be both heart-wrenching and uplifting at the same time."

She thought of the countless families that had come through for servings of chicken soup, sliced turkey, and a biscuit. Children with smudged cheeks and twinkling eyes. Single mothers grateful for a hot meal before their next stop at the local shelter. She felt appreciative of the many blessings she had in her own life, not the least of which were those that came with a roof over her head and food predictably on her table.

"So - this might be a stupid question, but - is the first 'F' in the six step plan 'Food'?" she asked.

"It's not a stupid question," he smiled, "and you're not crazy for wondering if that might be it," Elijah responded. "But no, it isn't. The first 'F' is *'Fulfillment'*."

"Fulfillment?" Casey looked puzzled.

"That's right," he said. "Did you know that the rate of depression and anxiety has been on a slow, steady increase in this country over the last 90 years?"

"Sadly, that's not surprising. Sometimes it feels like just about everyone is going through something," she answered. "So I imagine that's why everyone is in such a hurry to retire. They hate their jobs!"

"That might be true. Except for this:" he said, "according to some studies, retirement can increase the likelihood that a person will have depressive symptoms.[3]"

"What?" Casey was stunned. "How can that be? Don't people strive their whole lives to get to retirement? How is it that they are more likely to become depressed as a result?" she asked.

"Let me ask you something," Elijah said, "if you had all the free time in the world because you were no longer working long hours at your job, what would you do?"

She thought about it for a moment, "Do you mean with my free time? I'd relax - that's for sure! And I'd travel. I want to travel more than anything."

"Relaxing is nice," Elijah said, "and travel is wonderful. But realistically, how much relaxing and travel would you do? Even if you travel 20 weeks out of the year - which is a lot - what would you do with the other 32 weeks? You wouldn't just spend them all 'relaxing', would you?"

---

3 https://www.sciencedirect.com/science/article/abs/pii/
S0165178118301203?via%3Dihub

"When you put it that way, I suppose not," she answered. "Wow - I've never really thought about that. I'm enticed by the idea of being a Dollar Farmer to gain control of my time and do things like go on my father's family reunion cruise. But beyond that, I'm not sure what I'd do with my time."

"And by the way, there'd be lots and lots of time - if you do a good job building a Dollar Farm," he said.

He could see that she was battling inwardly - unsure of how to respond to the dilemma of having so much free time and not knowing how to fill it.

"So getting back to the idea of why people might get depressed in retirement: besides a paycheck, what do most people derive from their jobs?" Elijah posed.

"Besides frustration?!?"

They both laughed, then Casey thought about it a moment. "I suppose 'friendships'. People get to know other people at their jobs."

Elijah nodded, "That's right. That's one of the very important benefits that most people derive from work. There are others."

"I guess 'goals'. Things to strive for if you take pride in the work you do," she posited.

"Absolutely. Whether they're conscious of it or not, a job or career gives people a purpose. A reason to 'get up in the morning' so-to-speak," he replied. "And for most people, two very important ingredients to happiness and fulfillment are a sense of community and a sense of purpose."

"Otherwise," she added rhetorically, "why are we even here?"

"So for many people, even if they think they hate their jobs - and they legitimately might - without them, they can lose two critical ingredients necessary for a happy life: *people and purpose*," Elijah said.

"Which is why people might become depressed after they retire," Casey said. She pondered it a bit more. "So you're worried that if I become a Dollar Farmer, I'll become depressed? That I'd lose my sense of community and purpose?"

"On some level, yes. Part of the ambition in becoming a Dollar Farmer is to create time for yourself. But a recent study by the American Psychological Association found that having too much free time can be just as damaging to your emotional health as not having enough of it.[4]"

"Wow," she exclaimed, "I wouldn't have ever considered that."

"So I want to take you back to the first 'F' I'd mentioned," he said.

"Fulfillment?" Casey asked.

"Yes. The entire purpose of becoming a Dollar Farmer is to achieve *Financial Freedom and Fulfillment*. Without *Fulfillment*, you may as well work a 50-hour a week job for the next 35 years. You'd be more likely to be happy than if you have all the free time in the world without having purpose and good people to help you fill it," he said.

"So how do I find 'Fulfillment'?" Casey asked. "I just kinda figured that if I had free time on my hands, I'd find fun ways to fill it."

"That's largely true - I don't want to negate the fun you'll find in recreation," Elijah added. "For example, you've seen me enjoy plenty of hobbies like playing golf and going to wine tastings."

"Yes - I'd make more time for painting and yoga," she said.

"That's wonderful! And I'm sure you will," he said. "But part of what makes those hobbies so enjoyable is that I'm able

4 https://www.apa.org/pubs/journals/releases/psp-pspp0000391.pdf

to dedicate as much time and energy to things that are very meaningful to me."

"Like volunteering at a soup kitchen," Casey added.

"Precisely." Elijah smiled at Casey, proud that she was understanding and embracing the lesson. "Having fun doing things you enjoy is great. But absent meaningful activities, a life of pure recreation or hedonism can eventually feel empty. And a life without anything or anybody in it will become depressing. The greatest joy any of us can derive is in living a life of service - one where we do our part, no matter how small, to leave the world a little better than we found it."

"So I need to find ways I can contribute and give back?" she asked.

"Yes. And it'll be wonderful for you to have money to donate. But more rewarding will be the ways that you can invest your time - your newly liberated free time - towards causes you find important," he said. "And as importantly, think of all the wonderful things you'll do - recreationally as well - with your free time."

He continued, "I have a couple of assignments for you before we move on to the next 'F'. First, I want you to ponder the 4 'W's."

"Oh boy, Elijah," Casey exclaimed, "First there's 6 'F's and now 4 'W's! You really have created systems!"

He laughed, "That's right! And like I said earlier, having these little systems makes things easier to remember and easier to put in place. So step one of the 4 'W's: Identify your 'Who', 'What', 'When', and 'Where'." She looked at him intently before he continued, "'Who' will you enjoy spending your time with? 'What' will you do with your time? 'When' will you do the things you look forward to? And 'Where' will you live and visit?"

Her brain started racing with visions of things she'd do with her fiance, her family, and friends.

Elijah continued, "Your assignment for the next few days is to make a "Vision List". It's a list of the dreams, goals, hobbies, and causes that you'll be able to sink your free time into."

"It's interesting that you said the 4 'W's are 'Who', 'What', 'When', and 'Where'," Casey observed. "Those always seem to be accompanied with 'Why' but you left that one out."

"You're very astute, Casey," he said, "'*Why*' is the reason for the other 4 'W's: It will be paramount for you to have an underlying 'why' to help motivate you through the difficult time and work it will take to become a Dollar Farmer. Knowing your 4 'W's along with the next bit I'm going to ask you to do will help you find your 'Why' - or in reality, your many 'Whys'."

He leaned in, "Because - *and this is very important for you to remember* - becoming a successful Dollar Farmer will require tremendous patience and tenacity - far more so than going to work each week. And there will be times when you want to quit and just go back to your comfortable 40-hour-a-week- job. That's when this list will be most important. It will reinvigorate you and inspire you," he said.

"So what needs to be on the list?" she asked.

"I want you to break it down into three parts:

1. Bucket List
2. Daily Recreation
3. Meaningful Contributions"

She wrote those items down.

He explained, "The first item, a 'Bucket List' is your set of dreams of things you'd like to 'be, have, or do' before you kick the proverbial bucket. Before you die. They don't usually happen overnight and aren't necessarily going to happen more than once."

"Like diving in the 'Great Barrier Reef' in Australia." Casey said.

"Excellent! That goes on your Bucket List. Anything that is a big picture, maybe once in a lifetime dream or goal goes there," he said. "And it's a list I'd strongly encourage you to write with your significant other. You'll be amazed at how impactful it will be for you both to align on this."

"That sounds exciting!" Casey remarked.

"Next, put together a list of things you enjoy doing regularly," Elijah said.

"Like travel?" Casey asked.

He shook his head, "Not quite - travel is in the 'Bucket List' category, especially when you identify specific travel. For example, going to the 'Great Barrier Reef' or visiting the 'Grand Canyon'. I want you to get specific. The word 'travel' is too vague. Besides, travel is something you'll enjoy doing but not necessarily 52 weeks out of the year," he said. "For the 'Daily Recreation' section, I want you to identify activities that you'll enjoy doing with your regular free time. For me, those include writing, surfing, golf, and enjoying fine art. I think you'd mentioned painting and yoga earlier, is that right?"

She nodded, "Yes, I've always enjoyed painting. I just don't have much spare time to do it."

"Great! That's exactly the kind of thing you'd put here: things like painting and yoga that you can do each day or a few times a week. Basically, activities you'll enjoy that will keep you from having too much idle time," Elijah said.

"Otherwise, we become couch potatoes," she laughed.

"And depressed," he added. "And lastly, and here's where you'll find the most 'meaning': make a list of causes that inspire you. For me, it's volunteering each week at the soup kitchen. I also spend time mentoring at-risk kids. Nothing brings me more joy."

Casey lit up, "I love working with kids too. My niece spent time in a children's hospital when she was younger. Helping the kids there would make me so happy."

"There you go," he smiled. "Now for each of these items - Bucket List, Daily Recreation, and Meaningful Contribution - start to identify the 4 'W's that you'd enjoy these activities with. For example, 'with *Who*' and 'by *When*' would you want to go to the 'Great Barrier Reef'? A response - and this is just my example for you - is, 'I'd like to go to the Great Barrier Reef with my fiance by the time I'm 40 years old.'"

"Wow, that is specific," Casey said.

"It is. And you may not have all 4 'W's for every activity. But the more specificity you can bring, the better it will help you visualize it. And visualization is an important ingredient to both help keep you motivated and place you on a path towards actualization. When we cast our specific visions into the Universe, we are far more likely to make them a reality."

"That sounds a bit 'New Age-y'," Casey rebutted.

Elijah shrugged his shoulders, "It might. But it's also true. Writing out our dreams and goals while visualizing them helps make them come true because it gives our psyche and our will something to train their energy towards. It's like circling a destination on a map before starting a journey. Without a destination, you'll wander aimlessly."

"But if you are specific about where you are traveling, you are more likely to get there," Casey surmised.

"Bingo!" he exclaimed. "Most importantly, though, it will help you on the path towards 'Fulfillment'. Do you see why this first 'F' is so important?"

"Yes," she replied, "without 'Fulfillment', there's no purpose in working towards financial freedom."

"And without the promise of 'Fulfillment', you may lose the energy and nerve towards working for it in the first place," he added.

"Thanks, Elijah. I'm ready to start working on my 3 lists: bucket list, daily recreation, and meaningful contributions along with the 4 'W's."

"Fantastic. When you're done with that, we can get to work on the next 'F'," he said.

"I'm looking forward to it," Casey acknowledged with a twinkle in her eye.

**TO DO** | Create your own "Vision List" by following Elijah's example. Visit our website, www.TheDollarFarmer.com to use the template there or create your own. Create a "Bucket List", i.e., things you'd like to do before you "kick the bucket"; a "Daily Recreation" list, i.e., things you enjoy doing with your free time, and; a "Meaningful Contributions" list, i.e. service-oriented activities and causes that you'd like to lend your time, energy, and efforts to. These count as the first of the "4 W's" - the "What" you will do with your time.

Then, add specificity by completing the remaining "3 W's" to each of the activities: "Who do I want to enjoy these activities with", "Where will these activities take place?", and "(By) When will these activities take place?"

### Chapter 5

# The Flowing River

"How'd your homework go?" Elijah asked.

"I've got to be honest, Elijah: I'm inspired and energized. My fiance Jake and I mapped out a dream board and made a list of all the things you said. I don't think I've ever been this excited for my future. Thank you," she answered. "Can I share it with you?"

"Of course!" he nodded. "In fact, sharing it with people who are cheerleaders for your success will help you move towards your dreams and goals. But the reverse is also true - sharing your vision board with people who don't have your best interests at heart can be very damaging and detrimental."

"How do you mean?" she asked.

"Many if not most people will have a difficult time accepting your vision for a fulfilled life and future. And those same people might try to derail you with negativity. I call them energy parasites. Like weeds and pests on a real farm, they can eat away at your energy and destroy your efforts as a Dollar Farmer. You have to be very careful not to let energy parasites onto your Farm."

She thought carefully about some of the people in her life and knew he was right. There were several people she considered 'friends' who she knew would try to undermine her efforts as a Dollar Farmer if she shared her vision board with them.

He continued, "But people who truly have your best interests at heart will help keep you inspired and motivated. And when they question some of your actions or efforts, it will be because they genuinely care and are trying to help rather than because they are trying to undermine you. Learn to know the distinction between the two types of people and share your goals judiciously."

"Thank you," she smiled and opened her dream board to Elijah, knowing that he was one on the right side of that distinction. Her board looked like this:

**BUCKET LIST**

| WHAT DO I WANT? | WITH WHO? | WHERE? | BY WHEN? |
| --- | --- | --- | --- |
| Celebration Cruise | My whole family - especially my Dad | The Mediterranean | This coming November |
| Diving in the Great Barrier Reef | Jake | Australia | By the time I'm 35 |
| Yoga Retreat | Girlfriends | Hawaii | Next Fall |
| Dream Home | Jake | Springfield | 2 years |
| Trip to Israel | Jake & Family | Israel | 5 years |
| Learn to surf | Jake and friends | Cocoa Beach | By Age 30 |
| Dive the Galapagos | Scuba Team | Galapagos Islands | By Age 38 |

## DAILY RECREATION

| WHAT DO I WANT? | WITH WHO? | WHERE? | BY WHEN? |
| --- | --- | --- | --- |
| Yoga sessions 5x each week | New yoga partners | My yoga studio | Next year |
| Regular Painting sessions | Just me | Home studio | Within 6 months |
| Weekly 'Date Night' | Jake | On the town! | Right away |
| Read a book each week | Myself | At the park and home | Right away |

## MEANINGFUL ACTIVITIES

| WHAT DO I WANT? | WITH WHO? | WHERE? | BY WHEN? |
| --- | --- | --- | --- |
| Volunteer for the Children's Hospital | Jake | The Children's Hospital | Monthly starting ASAP |
| Do a beach and park cleanup | Friends | Local parks and beaches | Monthly starting ASAP |
| Visit Mom & Dad and record their life story | Myself | Parents' House | Start this week |

He smiled, "That's wonderful. Keep that energy going and remember, during the weeks and months that you're building your Dollar Farm, keep revisiting it. The inspiration will help you plow forward."

"Speaking of 'plowing forward'," Casey said, "does us sitting by this river have anything to do with the next lesson?"

"It does," Elijah answered. The pair sat at a lush riverbank across from an old, wooden water wheel. Its timeless spokes caught the water as the wheel turned with the rhythmic flow of the rushing stream.

"Tell me, Casey, what does that water wheel do?" Elijah asked.

She shrugged her shoulders, "I'm not sure. On a basic level, I see it turning as the river pushes against it. But I'm not sure if that's what you're asking."

He nodded, "Yes, on a basic level, that's the most important thing to observe. Going a little bit deeper, its function is to create electricity by transforming the kinetic energy of the turning spoke into electrical energy. That process creates what is generally known as 'hydropower'."

"You learn something new every day," Casey smiled.

"What do you suppose would happen if the river's flow stopped?" Elijah asked.

"The wheel would stop turning. And then it would stop making electricity," she replied.

He nodded, "That's right. Without the water flow, the entire process would stop."

"I imagine that somewhere in there is the lesson we'll be learning today, right?" Casey asked.

Elijah smiled, "You are catching on to my ways pretty quickly. In our first lesson, we didn't talk about money, per se."

"No," she added, "it was about 'Fulfillment'. About ways we can go about seeking and achieving a fulfilling life."

"Correct," he said. "Today, though, I do want to pivot to Dollar Farming in general and money more specifically. Let me ask you Casey, is money important?"

"Well, there's the old adage, 'money can't buy love or happiness'. So I try not to give money itself too much energy. I'm not materialistic if that's what you're asking," Casey answered.

"You took the question from a personal perspective which I understand. And I sense you may feel I would have judged you negatively if you'd answered that it was. But I'm genuinely asking at the most basic, fundamental level," Elijah continued, "is money important?"

Casey blushed before answering, "Of course it is." Casey reflected a moment before continuing, "I've thought a lot about our first conversations. About when we talked about humanity having evolved from our state as 'hunters and gatherers'. Back then, there was no money - what we did was collect what we needed to survive. As we became farmers, we developed trades and crafts. So I imagine we originally bartered with each other. I'm no anthropologist but I can envision someone trading a dozen eggs for wool. Or exchanging apples for tools, for example."

Elijah listened with the loving pride of a parent as Casey spoke. She said, "And I suppose that somewhere along the way, bartering became inefficient so we created currency as an easier way to barter. Maybe gold and silver coins at first. Eventually paper bills. Now, digital information in bank accounts. But it's money - money is the currency we use to pay for all the things we need in life. And unless we go back to some form of barter system, then yes - money is very important."

He nodded, "Bravo, Casey. I couldn't have expressed any of that better than you just did." She smiled in appreciation. He said, "Answer me this, then: is there anything that doesn't cost money? Anything at all?"

She thought about it for a moment, "Maybe only the air we breathe."

He smiled and shook his head slowly, "I'd actually disagree. Even the air we breathe has a cost."

"What do you mean?" she asked.

Elijah explained, "Aren't there regulations in place to make sure our air is kept clean and breathable? So that companies and industries don't pollute it?"

"Yes," she answered, "but we don't pay for the air itself."

"Maybe not directly," he said, "but when you consider that companies need to spend money to comply with clean-air regulations, where do you think those added costs show up?"

"In the price of the things they make?"

Elijah nodded, "Exactly. So while you don't directly pay for the air you breathe, in some ways, we still pay to have clean air. And by the way - that's a good thing. I'm happy that our society values a clean environment. But I was just trying to emphasize the bigger point."

"That everything has a financial cost," Casey added.

"So we've arrived at a bottom line of sorts: *life costs money*. Living has 'expenses'. And those expenses need to be paid for continually with money," Elijah said. "Why is there a need for the 'earned' income that Dollar Hunters and Dollar Gatherers work for? Or the 'passive' dollars that Dollar Farmers harvest?"

"Because if the income stops, then life's expenses can't be paid for," she answered.

"That's right," he agreed. "We need a constant income stream. You've heard that phrase before, haven't you?"

"Income stream?" Casey asked. "Of course."

"Speaking of 'streams'," Elijah pointed back at the running river and the water wheel, "What is it that makes the wheel turn?"

Casey replied, "The stream. *The flowing river*."

He smiled and nodded as if to prod her forward.

"Flow," Casey lit up, "the next 'F' is 'Flow'!"

"Yes!" Elijah exclaimed, "Tell me what you're thinking."

"Without water flow, the wheel will not turn and there will be no electricity. So in financial terms, without money 'flowing' in, there's no way to pay for the monthly expenses that life costs us!" she said.

"There is another very common financial term you may be familiar with that expresses this concept," he said.

"Is it 'Cash Flow'?" Casey asked.

"Exactly," Elijah said. "In simple terms, '*Cash Flow*' is the relationship between money coming in versus money going out. Financial people might describe it as 'income minus expenses'. Positive cash flow means you've got more money coming in each month or each year than you spend. Negative cash flow means you spend more than is coming in," he explained. "So the key for you is to understand that the underlying need is to *create sustainable, positive cash-flow*, that is, more money coming in than you spend or need."

Elijah gave her a moment to process what he'd said before continuing, "That might seem like an obvious concept but the truth is, it's easy to let Cash Flow slide as life happens. So I want you to always mind your 'flow'. If you're getting into financial difficulties, it's likely that your flow has started to slide. That more is going out than is coming in."

Casey nodded.

"Now that we've established that life costs money," he said, "we must find consistent income to pay for it because if we don't..."

"The wheel will stop turning," Casey finished.

"Yep. Normally," Elijah said, "people go to work to earn a paycheck. That paycheck constitutes the income that is used to pay for the expenses."

"That's what makes them '*Dollar Gatherers*'," Casey said.

"Correct. What we're hoping to do is find other sources of regularly recurring income that can - over time - replace the paycheck. In keeping with the river analogy, we want to build a 'stream' of income. Or, as we've been discussing, plant a 'dollar farm'," he said.

"But before doing that," he continued, "I wanted to just start the process of having you understand 'Flow'. Over the course of your lifetime as a 'Dollar Farmer', you'll need to make sure your Farm is providing regularly recurring income in the same way that the stream's flow continually pushes the wheel."

Casey answered, "I understand. I must plant a farm that will produce income over and over."

"And," Elijah said, "you must assure that the income will continue to persist to meet your regular expenses. So I've got your homework for this week."

"Ugh - I hate homework!" Casey laughed.

"Your last assignment was inspiring, wasn't it?" Elijah smiled. Casey nodded. "We'll break this into two parts. First, you need to identify what your lifestyle costs you now on a monthly basis. I want you to take a look at everything you and Jake regularly spend your money on to enjoy the life you have and break it down. That includes everything: your housing, your transportation, groceries, utilities, and entertainment. Put it all down on a spreadsheet. Then, split those expenses into 'needs' and 'wants'."

"So as an example," Casey said, "buying groceries is a 'need' but going out for an expensive dinner at a nice restaurant is a 'want'."

"Exactly. It's going to be important to know what your 'survival' cost is compared to your 'lifestyle' cost. Then," he continued, "I want you to look at the list you'd made from the prior assignment for 'Fulfillment' and determine what your future desired lifestyle is going to cost you."

She answered, "So let me make sure I understand: First, I need to know what my basic necessities for living cost currently. Then, I need to know how much more it costs for my life including 'fun' things. And lastly, I need to identify how much life will cost once we reach our 'Fulfillment' goals."

"You got it. It's going to be paramount that we start building your Dollar Farm to meet each of these thresholds in steps. Remembering that none of it will occur overnight, having these income plateaus to build towards will be incredibly helpful," he finished.

"Consider it done," Casey smiled. "Jake and I will get to work on this right away."

ASSIGNMENT | Create a breakdown of your current monthly expenses. Use the spreadsheet on our site, www.TheDollar-Farmer.com or create your own. Categorize your expenses as either "needs" or "wants".

Then, follow Casey's example by pricing out your future desired lifestyle by revisiting your 'Fulfillment' assignment. This will help you plan strategically for your life as a Dollar Farmer.

## Chapter 6

# Standing On Solid Ground

The next week, Casey and Elijah spent the day volunteering for an organization that builds homes for underprivileged families. After eight exhausting - and rewarding hours, Elijah took Casey to a family-owned diner for a much deserved meal.

"How was the day for you?" Elijah asked.

"Really tiring. But I also enjoyed it a bunch," Casey smiled. "This felt a lot like our day volunteering in the soup kitchen. Very fulfilling."

"Great! I'm happy you felt that way," he said. "It's always important to keep refueling our 'Fulfillment' tank."

They took a bite of their meals before he continued, "And were you able to complete your homework assignment? To map out your lifestyle expenses?"

She nodded, "Yep. It was a lot less fun than the 'Fulfillment' homework! But it was also very enlightening. It's humbling to see how much money we spend on 'junk'!"

"Spending money on 'junk' as you call it, is a luxury we have when we have extra discretionary income. I imagine you and your fiance both earn a nice living," Elijah said, "And there's nothing wrong, by the way, to enjoy the fruits of your labor."

"A-ha! A farming analogy," Casey remarked.

"You're right - though no pun was intended," Elijah smiled. "What is important is that your spending remains within reason and that you keep an eye on your 'Flow'. That you don't regularly spend beyond your means."

"My fiance Jake realized that we basically spend what we earn. If there's an extra dollar at the end of the month, we find a way to spend it," she said.

"That's not uncommon, by the way. These can sometimes be difficult lessons. But if you want to achieve financial freedom and fulfillment, they are also lessons you must master," he replied. "So what did you come up with - in regards to your current 'survival' expenses and 'desired lifestyle' expenses?"

"We found that our monthly costs just to 'survive' - no frills or thrills - is about $4000 each month," Casey answered.

"And did you categorize that so that you have a sense of where the money goes?"

She nodded, "We broke it down into basic categories like housing, transportation, groceries, utilities, etc. We also realized that while $4000 isn't an insignificant amount of money, it's also a number that is easily within our current combined income."

"So to be clear," Elijah said, "if you had $4000 of income each month, you'd be able to 'survive', that is, keep a roof over your head, food on the table, and the lights on, so-to-speak."

Casey nodded, "That's right. It wouldn't be an exciting lifestyle but we would be ok."

"Great!" Elijah replied, "That'll make the first step of your life as a Dollar Farmer easier to step up to. And what about your 'desired lifestyle'? Did you come up with a number for that?"

"Do you mean our current desired lifestyle? Or our future dream board?"

He shook his head, "I'm not too concerned about your future dream board just yet. That will be something you and your partner can work on and share together. For now, I'm more interested in knowing whether you have a sense of how much it would cost for you and your fiance to enjoy your current desired lifestyle. Doing the things you enjoy like going out for dinner or going to the theater, for example."

She smiled, "Yes, we realized that we very much enjoy the 'finer things in life'. Our total desired lifestyle is actually about $8,000 each month! That was a big eye opener for us. So we actually took the extra step and broke it down into future levels. If we had $5000 a month - just a thousand dollars more than our 'survival income' - it would allow us certain creature comforts. Another $1500 gets us more fun and pleasure. And the extra $1500 is the icing on top!"

Elijah applauded, "Kudos! So now you'll have something to work for as you become a Dollar Farmer in basic financial increments. You now know that the first mountain to climb - to know you've achieved an important 'income replacement' threshold will be to earn $4000 each month in 'Farmed Income'. Another way of saying it is that by having $4000 each month from your Dollar Farm, you and your fiance will have enough financial security to 'survive'."

"Yes! That's what he and I realized. And that's the first number we can set as a goal. Then, we build to the next plateau of $5000 each month and so on," she added.

He nodded in agreement, "That's right. Now, I should emphasize that the first threshold certainly won't happen overnight. Or at least, it isn't likely to. You won't reach the $4000 number the first month you start farming. In fact, when I started my life becoming a Dollar Farmer, I was working in a very comfortable and secure employment position and my farming ventures were very time consuming with very little to show for it. I remember the first bit of income I received from one of my farming ventures was a mere $80 of monthly income. But that was a very important milestone: I looked at my expenses and saw that for me, it covered the cost of my TV Cable bill."

Casey's face went blank before looking down.

"What's wrong?" he asked.

She pondered it a moment before saying, "I realize all this time you've been saying that this would be a long process. That it would take hard work and time so I had accepted that. But," she paused as he listened, "just now as you said, $80 per month from your first farming venture..." her voice trailed off.

He sat back and smiled, "You realized it's going to be a lot longer and perhaps harder than you'd allowed yourself to believe."

She nodded. "I just realize how desperately far I am from $4000 of farmed income each month. Financial Freedom? It seems like a pipe dream right now."

"Casey," Elijah said, "you're absolutely right. This will take a lot of time and effort. And at first, you and Jake might feel like it's absolutely not worth it. And that's why I told you to start with *'Fulfillment'*. *Because without having dreams to work for and an underlying 'why', you'll give up on it too easily* ."

He leaned in and continued, "And you'll readily go back to your comfort zone. Before you know it, you'll wake up at 60 years old having traded decades of your life for dollars wondering where it all went and with a list of things you wished you'd done."

She thought about his words and they spun her back to what started this all: missing her family's cruise and spending time with her terminally ill father. She thought about the life he and her mom had together and how they'd worked so hard to reach 'retirement' without having enjoyed all those years while he was in a career. And she knew Elijah was right. As hard as it would be, it was the only way for her life to be 'her own'.

She nodded. "You're right. This is going to be hard work. And it's going to take time. But I'm willing. I must do it...."

He gave her a loving, compassionate smile, "So I bet you're wondering what the next step is, right?"

She smiled, "Yes - I want to build my dollar farm. *I must build my dollar farm.*"

"Good. Behind the fleeting moment of understandable anxiousness, I sense your determination. And determination will be critical."

"So what's next?"

"WHAT CAN YOU TELL me about what we did today, Casey?" he asked.

She grinned, "I figured the next lesson would somehow tie back to our work today. Well," she reflected, "we volunteered to build a home for an under-privileged family. On the most basic level, we came together to build a home for a single mom and her kids."

Elijah nodded, "That's right. And putting aside for a moment the feeling of 'fulfillment' you may have gotten from volunteering your time and energy, what did you learn about building a home?"

"That it's exhausting, hard work!" Casey laughed. He joined her with a laugh of his own. She continued, "And that it's methodically planned out - that there's a blueprint to it all."

"That's absolutely true - a house could not be built without a master plan. Or to be more precise, a quality, dependable house could not be built without a blueprint," Elijah concluded.

"Is that what we're getting at? That to build my dollar farm, I need a blueprint?" Casey asked.

"A blueprint for your dollar farm is very helpful for sure," Elijah said. "In many regards, that's what all of these lessons collectively are working towards - giving you a blueprint of sorts so that you and Jake can reach financial freedom and fulfillment."

"But that's not what *this lesson* is about," Casey recognized. "You're looking for something more specific."

Elijah nodded.

"Let's see," she said, "we started with '*Fulfillment*', which meant finding an underlying reason - a 'why' to help keep us focused towards our goal. Then, we learned about '*Flow*' - understanding the relationship between income and expenses and identifying how much income we'll eventually need to replace with 'farmed' dollars to enjoy our desired lifestyles without having to 'hunt or gather' our dollars at a traditional 'job'."

Elijah smiled. He saw she was understanding the lessons and beginning to apply them.

"You'd also said that there were '6 F's' and that 'Farming' would be the 4th. So there's one that today's lesson should help bridge the gap between 'Flow' and 'Farming'. Something about building a home...." Casey's voice trailed off as she contemplated what Elijah might be trying to teach her.

"Don't beat yourself up, Casey. This stuff isn't easy or obvious. But it is intentional," Elijah said. "Let's go back to 'process'. What did we do today?"

Casey was growing inwardly frustrated. "We built a house."

"That's right," Elijah said. "How did we do that?"

"We looked at the plan, gathered our materials, and started working together to build," she answered.

"You're right - but you're getting ahead of yourself. Take it more slowly," he whispered.

"I'm not sure what we're driving at, Elijah," she said, flustered a bit now.

He smiled, "Did we start with the roof? Or painting the walls?"

She shook her head. She started to sense where he was going, "Of course not. You can't start with a roof."

"Why not?"

"Because there's nothing for it to rest on," she answered. "'Floor'," she said, "we start with a 'Floor'. That's the 3rd 'F'."

He smiled, "You're very close, Casey. And yes - we'd need a floor before we could put up walls and then a roof. But there's something important - in fact, something critical that comes before the floor, isn't there?"

She blushed at how suddenly obvious the answer felt and how she could have overlooked it. "'*Foundation*'," she nodded, "we have to build a 'Foundation'."

Elijah leaned back, proud of his student and her ability to synthesize the information she was learning.

"Without a foundation, the house will be unstable and could come crumbling down at any moment," she added. "So we need to build a solid foundation for our Dollar Farm, right?"

"Yes," he said, "that's exactly right. Now that you have an eye towards '*Fulfillment*' and an understanding of '*Flow*', we must lay a solid '*Foundation*' before we start '*Farming*'." They took a moment to enjoy a bit of their meals before he continued. "Dollar Farming is rewarding and will ultimately allow you the opportunity to use your time and plan your life in the manner you choose rather than the manner in which an employer chooses. However," he paused, "before that occurs, you will have to plant, till, sow, and harvest your income farm. And - especially in the early stages - farmed income is minimal at first and often unpredictable."

"I thought you'd said that farmed income would be predictable and recurring - that the idea of it was that I'd know how much income was coming in each year before the year even started," she rebutted.

"That's largely true but only after you've reached a point of critical mass - and that can take time," he answered. "Initially, it is largely unpredictable. Think of it this way - when you plant a fruit tree, in its infancy, it won't bear any fruit. You'll have to keep working it," Elijah said.

"And have other sources of food in the meantime," she added.

"Correct," he said, "then, once it starts to mature, those early harvest years will not always bring sufficient or predictable harvests. Some years, you'll be pleasantly surprised - others, you'll be disappointed."

"So I need to be sure that until my Dollar Farm is generating sufficient income, I have to have other sources of income to keep food on the table and a roof over my head," Casey said.

"Yes," Elijah smiled, "Or - sufficient resources to bridge gaps."

"Resources? Gaps?" she asked.

"That's right. Look at it this way: imagine you've established enough 'farmed' income to replace your $4000 monthly 'survival' need. You and Jake decide to shift - or even quit your full-time jobs since you have enough income to get by," he said.

"Wow - that's exciting just thinking about it!" Casey exclaimed.

"It would be. But then - like the fruit tree example I gave earlier - you have a month or two where your sources of farmed income aren't yet reliable or mature. And you only receive $1500 of income. You'd have a shortfall or a 'gap'," Elijah explained. "What would you do then?"

"I'm not sure," she pondered. "I guess I've always taken for granted the fact that Jake and I each make good money - there's always more than enough to get by and then some."

"Trust me, with farmed income - that won't be assured - at least not in the beginning. As a general matter, whether you were looking to become a Dollar Farmer or remain a Dollar Hunter / Gatherer," he continued, "you should always maintain 'reserve funds' to protect against 'cash flow gaps' or unexpected expenses."

"Is that what some people call an 'emergency account'?" Casey asked.

Elijah nodded, "Yes - that's one name it goes by. I've heard others use the expression, 'rainy-day fund'. You can call it whatever you want - the name isn't what matters. What is important is that you have reserves - like a squirrel who hoards nuts for winter - to help you through 'flow gaps'. And you need to build those reserves before you start your dollar farm."

"I get it," she said, "How much do we need to save? And how do we do it?" she questioned.

"Let's start with the second question first," Elijah said. "Currently, you and Jake both have good jobs with reliable incomes, right?"

Casey nodded.

"And you mentioned that you basically spend what you earn - even though it's a lot more than what you *need* to live on?" he asked.

She blushed, "Yeah, we do. I'm not proud of it but the truth is that we probably make twice as much as we need to live on - and still spend all of it."

"Don't beat yourself up - that's why we're here: to help you get ready for this next and very exciting chapter of your financial life - and to help you build true financial freedom," he consoled.

"Now, I have to ask you an important question."

She braced herself for something she instinctively felt would be difficult.

"If both of you suddenly lost your jobs, how long would you get by on your current savings?" he asked.

"Ha! Maybe 20 minutes," she laughed. "Like I said, I'm not proud of it but we don't have very much set aside."

"Ok, and how would you manage - how would you pay the bills if your income stopped overnight?" Elijah continued.

"I guess we'd have to borrow the money. We'd probably have to use credit cards to pay our bills," she said dryly.

He nodded knowingly, "Yes - that's how many households get by. In that regard, you're not alone."

"But it's a pretty flimsy foundation," Casey acknowledged. "Gosh, I never realized how irresponsible we were."

"The reality is that you and Jake are not in a desperate situation - you both have good incomes and it's unlikely that you'd both suddenly lose your jobs from one day to the next. But...."

"But stranger things have happened. Like if we got into a car accident and both suddenly couldn't work," Casey interrupted. "And if we want to start a dollar farm, at some point, we will be letting go of one - then maybe both of our paychecks."

"That's right. The reality is that it's important to have a reserve account - an emergency fund or rainy-day account as you might call it," Elijah said. "And since you mentioned credit cards as the way you'd fund any shortfalls - do you currently carry any credit card debt?"

Casey looked down sheepishly. "We do. About $10,000 on a credit card."

"It's nothing to sneeze at. But it's nothing to be ashamed about either," Elijah said - letting her off the hook a bit. "You know, one of the great tragedies in our educational system is that a child can go from Pre-K to a PhD without ever taking a course on personal finance. It's no wonder that most people go through their entire adult lives without a good sense about how to handle money, savings, investments, or debt. So - as I've kept repeating - don't beat yourself up. We're going to take care of this."

She exhaled feeling a bit lighter but still without a sense of how to move forward. "So how do I go about building my 'Foundation'? I want to make sure I build my Dollar Farm on solid ground."

## Chapter 7

# A Leap Of Faith

"Earlier, you asked me two questions at once: how much do we need to save and how do we do it?" Elijah said. "The truth is, the answer to both questions is: 'it's up to you'."

"I'm not sure I follow," Casey said.

"I'd said that we should start by answering the 2nd question first - 'how do we do it?', and then we took a bit of a detour in our conversation," Elijah explained. "But that's ok - it gave us an opportunity to shed important light on ideas that will matter going forward. But the 'how you do it' is quite simple: rather than spend all you earn, you set some aside each paycheck. You develop a habit that no matter what, *the first part of what you earn is for you to save* - the rest is what you get to spend."

She looked at him quizzically, "I'm not sure what you mean by that."

He smiled, "There's a saying that many financial professionals use: '*Pay Yourself First*'. In other words, with every paycheck that comes in, before paying your bills or going out for drinks and dinner, you take a portion of that paycheck and put it aside. In that way, you won't have an opportunity to spend it."

"Or waste it," she added.

He smiled, "Let me tell you about myself when I was a bit younger. When I was in my early 20s, I had dreams then of being a music producer. At the time, I was waiting on tables and bartending to earn my money. Each shift, I'd make between $100 on a bad night to $250 on a good night. I'm not sure how much waiters or bartenders make these days but that's what my shifts were like."

Elijah took a sip of his iced tea before continuing, "My goal at that time - my *'why'* - was to build a home recording studio. The kicker was that it would cost ten thousand dollars - not small potatoes for a 23 year old kid who was determined to do it on his own. So every night, after my shift, I'd take a twenty dollar bill from the tips I'd earned and slip it into my sock drawer before I had a chance to blow it somewhere else. And - if it was a pretty good night - *or a really good night* - I'd pull another twenty dollar bill or two to add to the drawer. I figured the only way I'd ever be able to buy and build my recording studio was if I made some of what I earned 'sacred'. That I'd have to make some of the money I earned 'untouchable'. And the only way to do that was to set it aside before I had a chance to spend it."

"You paid yourself first," Casey smiled at Elijah. She saw the determination he'd had even as a young man to identify a goal and work towards it. She thought about the life she and Jake were building together and wondered for a moment if they had the same level of discipline.

"Pretty soon," Elijah continued, "the sock drawer started filling with cash. And the more I saved, the easier it became to put aside bigger chunks towards my goal. Before I knew it - I'd saved the $10,000 I needed to buy and build my home recording studio."

"What came of it? Your dreams to be a music producer?"

she asked.

He laughed, "That's a story for another day - a lesson I will also share. But the lesson for you today is: *to build your Foundation, you must make a sacrifice.* And the more you're willing to sacrifice in the short term, the faster you'll build your Foundation."

"So the moral of the story is - if Jake and I are willing to sacrifice some of our current creature comforts and pleasures, we'll be able to build our Foundation. And the more we cut back, the faster we'll do it," Casey concluded. "So if we go into 'survival' mode - only live on what we need, we could get there in no time!"

"Yes….but…" Elijah started.

"What?" Casey asked, "I thought I'd nailed that: stop doing 'fun stuff' and save our cash!"

He laughed, "To an extent, yes - that's what I mean. But hear me out: I'd hate for you and Jake to suddenly go into 'survival' mode and not allow yourselves to ever enjoy any 'fun stuff'. At the risk of sounding morbid, life is short. You're still meant to enjoy it as it's happening and not in complete deferral to some future that may never arrive."

"Ok - now you've got me spinning - and a little annoyed, Elijah," Casey said. "We're in our 20s - I'm not worried at the moment of a future that may never arrive!"

"Fair point," he replied, "I just mean that you shouldn't suddenly go on a 'cat-food' diet!"

"Don't worry - Jake and I will still enjoy life and eat just fine. But we will be cutting back - at least until we've built our 'Foundation' - on some of our simple pleasures. Instead of expensive steakhouse dinners - we'll make steak at home!"

"Great," Elijah said. "And that's partly why I said earlier that it would be 'up to you'. The speed at which you save a portion of each paycheck will determine how quickly you create your savings 'Foundation'. The more you save from each paycheck, the faster you'll have built your reserves."

She nodded, "So if the first step is to take some of what I earn and set it aside, how will we know how much is the right amount?"

"Actually," Elijah said, "the first step is to pay off that credit card. A Dollar Farmer starts their farm debt free."

She looked down after hearing his response.

"What's the problem?" he asked.

"Debt free? Jake and I just bought a house. We have a $300,000 mortgage."

"My apologies - I should have been more specific. A home mortgage - if you have good terms - is completely acceptable and understandable. In fact, for most people, the only way they can get into their first home is to take out a mortgage. That's not what I was referring to."

"Thank God! I almost had a heart attack," she exclaimed.

He continued, "What I was talking about was consumer debt - particularly credit card debt. Credit cards can be a source of short-term cash and used correctly can serve to deliver various kinds of points and rewards you will ultimately take advantage of. But for too many people, they become an alternative to their reserve account. Pretty soon, credit cards with high interest rates work against positive 'Flow' and become an impediment to laying a solid 'Foundation'."

She understood his point. Casey knew that each month, she and her fiance paid a few hundred dollars towards the credit card and yet the balance never seemed to go down. It had never really bothered her since the bill was manageable for them. But she also realized how easily they had accumulated a five figure credit card balance. And that the expense was a slow creeping strain on their ability to gain independence.

She looked at Elijah and said, "I get it. As long as we use a credit card as a savings account, we can never be Financially Free because we are indebted. And the only way to get out of our debt is to reduce our spending and use the difference to knock down the debt."

"It is a great way. But it isn't the only way," Elijah answered.

"What do you mean?" asked Casey.

"This goes back to 'Flow'. 'Flow' is the difference between income and expenses; inflows vs outflows. So you said that the only way to reduce your credit card bill is to reduce your expenses in other ways and use the difference to pay down that credit card. That would work. But let me ask you: is there another way?"

She smiled, "Of course! If 'Flow' is the difference between income and expenses, then to increase my 'Flow', I can either reduce my expenses OR increase my income. If I can make more money, then I can use the extra I've made to pay down that credit card and eventually, start building my reserves."

"Exactly. Remember what I told you about what I did when I had an especially good shift," he said.

"Yep," she smiled, "you'd take an extra twenty dollar bill or two and put it in your sock drawer."

"That's right!" he responded.

"But Jake and I don't make 'extra money' at our jobs. We're on a salary. We're Dollar Gatherers," she remarked.

"That's true now - but as you start 'farming', you'll start generating more income. Those 'extra' farmed dollars can be used to pay down your credit cards or build your reserve," he explained.

"But I thought you said I shouldn't start farming until I already had my foundation built with proper reserves. And that I shouldn't build my reserves until my credit cards were paid off," Erica rebutted.

"I recognize how confounding some of this might seem," Elijah answered. "You're right - I've suggested that we wouldn't start farming until those things occurred. In reality, what I want is for you not to eliminate your existing sources of 'hunter / gatherer' income until you have built your reserves. In other words, don't quit your 'day-job' *yet*. I want you to have what we'd all agree is a 'steady paycheck' before you rely exclusively on 'farmed income'."

She smiled, "So you are saying that in my *spare time*, I can start farming anytime."

"That's right," Elijah agreed. "There's nothing that prevents you or Jake from 'hustling' to build your farm even while you still have your 'day jobs'."

"Gotcha," she said, "So step one is to use surplus cash flow by either increasing my income, decreasing my spending - or both - to pay off my credit card. Then, use that same surplus to start building my reserve account."

"Absolutely," Elijah answered. "Think of it this way: you and Jake can continue 'gathering' dollars from your reliable paychecks while in your spare time, you start creating your 'Dollar Farm'."

"And all the while, we're using our extra cash flow by cutting our expenses to pay off our credit card and then build our reserves," she smiled.

"Bingo," he exclaimed.

"Once we've paid off the credit card, how will we know how much we need in our reserve account? How will we know that we can quit our 'day jobs' and start 'farming' full time?" she asked.

Elijah sat back and pondered her question a moment. He knew what he was about to tell her wouldn't be easy to understand or accept. And yet, he was confident she'd be able to take the counsel in the manner he intended.

"Casey, the truth is, you won't necessarily ever know for sure," he said, "There is no exact number or amount I can tell you is the 'right' amount you should have in your reserve account. There are 'rules of thumb',￼" he continued, "Amounts that professional financial advisors and representatives 'suggest' that a person or household should keep in reserves. But in truth, that's all they are - 'rules of thumb'. "

She looked at him inquisitively, hoping he'd offer more specific guidance. He understood her apprehension and expanded upon what he'd been saying, "You and Jake will feel it - you'll know when the time is right. When you have 'enough' in reserves and cash-flow surplus to feel confident to stop your lives as 'Dollar Gatherers' so that you can focus your efforts exclusively as 'Dollar Farmers'. You'll know because you'll look at your reserve account and trust that if you have an income gap - or difficulties in getting your Dollar Farm up to speed, that there'll be sufficient money there to get you through without having to rely on credit cards or borrowing money. And the reason I say there's no 'exact number' is because no two Dollar Farmers are starting from the same place. You and Jake have a circumstance that is entirely unique to you and nothing like the next person becoming a Dollar Farmer. So the key is to understand that there will come a moment when you'll know you're ready. And when that moment comes, you must fearlessly take the plunge."

"Like a leap of faith," she countered. Elijah nodded. "It's so different from everything I was taught growing up. You know, 'get a degree in a good professional industry, get an internship, parlay that into a career, then work your way up the ladder, blah, blah, blah.' Now I'm taking a leap of faith into the unknown."

"You won't ever feel like you're ready to take that leap. You can't *know* that you're ready to fly, any more than a baby bird launching herself from a nest high atop a tree *knows* she won't fall. But when that time comes, you must take the leap. Otherwise, you may never be truly 'financially free'," he said.

"And my life will not be my own," she added. He nodded compassionately.

She thought about it for a moment, then asked, "You mentioned 'rules of thumb'. What do the 'experts' suggest that a person keep in reserves?"

"Again, it depends on the circumstance," he answered, "but in general, for a single income household, financial advisors suggest between 6 and 9 months worth of living expenses be kept in savings. For a dual income household, a little less is acceptable. But that guidance is generally for households who have no intention of 'quitting their day jobs'," he finished.

"So it's really advice for people who have 'dollar gathering jobs' and don't intend to ever quit gathering dollars at those jobs," she concluded.

"That's right. For you and Jake, the calculation might be a little different. And you can always consider that one of you might step away from your career before the other. Or you might decide that one of you will always continue to keep a salaried career. That is very much a personal, lifestyle choice for you to make with Jake," he said.

"But if one of us does that," she continued, "then in some ways, one of us would always be tied to that job or career."

He didn't say anything. He didn't need to. He knew that she already understood the answer and the reality of it.

"So what's next? I mean - I know I have to pay off that credit card and start building my reserves. But you said I could do that while I start 'Dollar Farming'. So….." she tailed off.

"So," he smiled, "let's learn how to farm dollars."

"It's time?" she asked.

"It's time."

# PART III

# "Sow"

"The way to get started is to quit talking and begin doing. "

—Walt Disney

## Chapter 8

# Remember Not To Forget

"Why are we doing this?" Elijah asked.

"Dollar Farming?" she answered.

He nodded, "Yes - what prompted our conversations in the first place?"

"I suppose it comes back to my wanting to have ownership over my own time. Ownership over my own life," she replied.

"And what is it about a traditional job or career that prevents that?" he asked.

"Because in a traditional job or career, you are required to make certain hourly, weekly, or annual commitments in exchange for a paycheck," Casey said.

"And?" he probed.

"And....you only get paid once for the work you do - whether it's an hourly wage or annual salary," she responded.

"And what do we call that?"

"Dollar Gathering," she smiled.

"Why is it 'Dollar Gathering'?" he asked.

"Because - like our ancestors who used to forage for food - they could only have as much food as they'd 'gathered' during their 'work session'. Much like an hourly or salaried employee only gets paid as they 'work' for that shift of time," she said.

"And what about hunters? Aren't they a part of the equation?" he nudged.

"Sure - our ancestors who relied on hunting for food would 'eat what they killed' - nothing more. We liken them to 'commissioned salespeople' who are paid once for a transactional sale of goods or services," she said.

"What's wrong with that - with hunting or gathering your income?"

"There's nothing inherently *wrong* about it. But we have to acknowledge that by relying on Dollar Gathering or Dollar Hunting for our income, we will have a tough time achieving financial freedom or fulfillment because we'll have to go out and complete another 'shift' of work or 'transactional sale' to receive more income."

"And how is that different from Dollar Farming?" he asked.

"With Dollar Farming, we create an income source..."

"Or sources...." he interrupted.

She smiled, "Or sources - plural - that can generate regularly recurring income as a result of labor that was done only once."

"Why do we compare it to farming?"

"Because like a fruit tree, once planted and cultivated, that tree can give fruit over and over and over for many seasons without having to be planted or cultivated again. One unit of 'work' pays repeatedly," Casey said.

"And what does that look like when we translate it to Dollar Farming?"

"It means creating or building something that pays over and over after the initial, hard work is complete."

He continued, "Can you give me an example or two?"

"Sure," she said, "a person purchases a condominium unit, renovates it - then rents it for monthly income. They don't have to re-purchase or re-renovate the unit over and over. But it still keeps paying from those initial efforts."

"Good," he nodded, "Any other examples?"

"A person writes a novel and publishes it. Then, when readers purchase it, the author gets paid with each sale without having to write it over again."

"And what's so good about that?" Elijah dug deeper.

Casey continued gently, "You have ownership over your life. Because you are not tied to a schedule or singular transaction to earn your income. There is predictability and security knowing that income will be coming irrespective of how you spend your time."

"Does that mean that you'll never have to work again?" he asked.

"Not at all - you'll still have to maintain your farm. And that will require work. But there'll be greater flexibility since you won't be on a specific time schedule."

They both sat back and took a moment to consider the conversation. Casey asked, "Why did you ask me those questions? Were you afraid that I hadn't been paying attention? Or that I didn't understand what we've been discussing?"

"Not at all," he answered. "I believe it's good practice to review. To restate not only 'what' we are doing but also 'why' we do it. It's very easy in life to lose sight of the forest for the trees. And so I wanted to be sure we were both pausing to reflect and see the big picture before we took the deep dive into our next conversations."

Casey nodded in agreement as she looked around at their surroundings. A cool breeze tinged with hints of orange and lilac combed through her hair while she enjoyed the view of the locale Elijah had brought them to: a working farm not too far from their own urban neighborhood that somehow felt as if it were a million miles away. They sat at a cafe picnic table on the property where they dined on a glorious brunch made of only ingredients grown and cultivated on the farm.

"This is a special place," she remarked. "It has a spiritual energy to it."

He nodded in agreement, "Yes it does. It's a family-owned farm that has been passed down over time. It's now in the hands of its 4th generation."

The buzzing of honey bees danced at marigolds nearby.

"There's a tremendous amount of bio-diversity here," he added. "But that wasn't always the case."

"What do you mean?"

"You see, they cultivate all sorts of crops and livestock here. Pigs, chickens, and sheep along with an array of all sorts of fruits and vegetables including oranges, of course."

She smiled as she took in a deep, sweet breath through her nose.

"But once upon a time," he continued, "this farm only cultivated oranges."

"That's interesting," she commented. "I wonder why that changed."

"That is precisely one of the reasons we're here as we start our deeper dive into Dollar Farming," he answered.

### Chapter 9

# The CASH Cow

"Consider for a moment," Elijah said, "all of the different kinds of crops and livestock we find here. Just take a look down at your setting to think about what went into making your meal."

She saw her plate - upon it a fresh spinach, tomato, and cheese omelet lined with 3 strips of bacon, an almond-flour buttered biscuit, and a glass of freshly squeezed orange juice. "Everything that's here is from this farm?" she exclaimed in awe.

"That's right," he said. "Now, before a farmer sets out, they must do several things to produce the best possible results."

"Aren't those 'Fulfillment, Flow, and Foundation'?" she asked.

He appreciated her perspective for a moment before responding, "Actually - that only refers to what you'll need to understand before reaching the '*Farming*' step. But for actual '*Dollar Farming*', there are a number of things you'll do before you earn your first farmed dollar." He took a sip of his juice before continuing. "Before I say more - I'll emphasize that I'm not an actual farmer. What I'm about to say is an overly simplified analogy to draw the connection between food farming and dollar farming. But the analogy - I believe - will be quite useful in your work to earn regularly recurring and predictable income.

"Regularly recurring and predictable income," she echoed. "Farmed dollars, in other words."

"That's right. So let's look at the 4 steps - as I've simplified them - for farming." He wrote on the back of a napkin:

1. Choose your crop
2. Arrange and prepare the land
3. Sow and cultivate the crop
4. Harvest

"These are the four basic - and simplified steps that a farmer takes to get from idea to fruit-in-hand, so-to-speak," he finished. "They are the same four steps you'll follow as a Dollar Farmer to create and harvest your income streams."

"I expect we'll spend a bit more time on each," she remarked.

"Of course," he answered, "that'll come shortly. But before we do, let's take a big picture look at the four steps and an interesting way you'll come to remember them."

Casey took a moment to look at his notes on the napkin: *Choose your crop, Arrange and prepare the land, Sow and cultivate the crop, and Harvest.* She thought for a moment about Elijah's penchant for useful tools that made things easy to remember such as the '6 F's' she'd learn for Dollar Farming of which she was on her 4th. And then, with another glance, it hit her. She looked back at Elijah and smiled, "Of course: *Choose, Arrange, Sow, Harvest.* It's an acronym: *C.A.S.H.*"

"Bravo!" he exclaimed jubilantly. "You're picking up on my methods! Very good, Casey. Now let's take a deeper dive to understand a bit more about each of those steps before we really get our hands dirty, so-to-speak."

"Is it ok if I take a stab at it?" she asked.

"Of course! That would be fantastic," he replied.

"Starting with 'choose', it is the farmer's job to decide what crop or livestock they'd like to cultivate," she said as she looked down on her plate of food, realizing that there was an almost endless set of options. "A farmer makes a selection or choice of what they'll eventually want to harvest. They might decide on oranges, for example. Or pigs. Then, they 'arrange the land' as you put it. 'Arrange' must mean to prepare the land and make sure that the conditions are optimal for whatever crop or livestock the farmer has chosen in step one. Once that step is completed, the farmer will 'sow the seed' or plant the crop in other words. They will care for the crop as it grows until they arrive at the final step: 'harvest' when they'll - pun intended - enjoy the fruits of their labor."

"Very good, Casey - I couldn't have summarized it any better myself," Elijah said. "You might also notice that quite a bit of work is involved in those first 3 steps before the farmer arrives at the 'harvest' step."

"Yes," she answered, "you've been very careful to remind me that this is not a 'get-rich-easy' scheme."

"That's right. Now looking at the 4 steps, how would you relate those to farming dollars? To creating recurring income sources?" he asked.

She pondered it for a moment, then said, "As it relates to 'choosing', you'd first have to decide what income opportunity you'd want to develop. For example, we've talked about things like rental real-estate as compared to writing a book or buying stocks. So that's where 'choose' comes into play.

"Correct," he said. "Keep going, Casey."

She continued, "Then, once you've 'chosen', you 'arrange'." She gave it some thought before realizing - this step seemed less obvious. "In the world of 'dollar farming', I suppose this is where you do your market, service, and product research. For example - if I'm going to buy a rental property, I should make sure I know what rental rates are, how the market is situated, and how much I'd need to invest in a property to bring it to market. On the other hand, if I'm selling T-shirts online, I'd want to know how the market looks. Who's buying shirts? What kinds of shirts are they buying? What's the going rate?" She looked at Elijah for affirmation.

He nodded, "Go on."

"Then, for 'Sow' - I'm guessing this is where the rubber meets the road. Where the rental property investor purchases and prepares the unit for rent. Where the author writes and publishes the book. Where the ATM machine investor buys and places their units. And where the web developer loads their site and places ads."

He sat back, impressed at her broad understanding of 'dollar farming' and how the C.A.S.H. process unfolds. He said, "Fantastic, Casey. In fact, I've heard you mention several 'Dollar Farming crops' such as web development and online t-shirt sales that we hadn't previously discussed."

"Jake and I have really been educating ourselves - trying to understand all the different ways we can earn farmed income. There are so many different choices out there. It's a bit overwhelming, really," she answered.

"Yes it is," Elijah agreed, "and the truth is that the number will only continue to grow. We live in an age that increasingly makes dollar farming more and more possible. Technology and the interconnected world we live in are expanding these opportunities.

But the good news is that for you and Jake, in step 1, you'll choose the right crop - or crops for your dollar farm," he smiled.

"Which will ultimately lead to the final step: 'harvest'. I guess it doesn't need much explanation but I suppose it's where we start to earn our income," she smiled.

"Yes," he said, "but beyond earning income - it will be an opportunity for evaluation. It will allow you to determine what and how you adjust. *Farming isn't a singular event - it is an ongoing process which will allow you to improve and optimize.* Remember - your initial harvests will likely be scarce. But they will be very instructive."

She smiled.

"So," he continued, "shall we start to explore the first step: 'choosing' the crops for your 'dollar farm'?"

## Chapter 10

# Bacon, Eggs, And Cheese

"Let's consider once again, the food we've had the pleasure of enjoying today," Elijah started. "What are some of the crops or livestock that have been grown and harvested here to prepare your meal?"

"Well, we've got eggs, bacon, spinach, tomatoes, and oranges," she considered. "And even nuts. Almonds were used to make the flour which made these biscuits."

"Not to mention the goat's milk that was used to make the cheese and butter we enjoyed. Like we said earlier - a lot of bio-diversity on this farm," Elijah added.

"There sure is," Casey responded. "How does that relate to income? And dollar farming?"

"Good - let's see if we can make a connection," he said. "As we think of them as food products, how would you categorize them? What are the broadest categories they'd fall into?" he prodded.

"There were fruits - like tomatoes," she winked, "and vegetables like spinach. There were eggs from the chicken and dairy from the goats. And of course, a pig gave its life for the bacon."

"That's right," he agreed, "and would you be able to place those into broad categories? In other words, to be less specific?"

"I suppose," she said. "I guess fruits & vegetables might fall into one category that we'll call 'plants' and livestock into another."

"That's great. I might add a third: products derived from one of the primary two. For example, eggs and dairy are derived from 'livestock'. In other words, you could have a chicken farm where the eggs - not the chicken themselves - are the 'crop', so-to-speak, isn't that right?" Elijah explained.

"Of course. So I guess that's 3 categories: 'plants', 'livestock', and 'byproducts'," she said.

He nodded, "And I'm certain that actual farmers would disagree with these classifications. But again - we're just trying to make a broad analogy."

"Understood."

"So when a farmer starts contemplating step one - 'choosing' what crop or livestock - they will consider what might be most appropriate given the conditions of their farm and the land they'll toil," Elijah explained. "This particular farm has made the 'choice' to be very diverse. We'll spend a good amount on the thinking behind that a little later in our conversation. But for now, let's consider that in step one, a farmer makes a choice about perhaps the 'broad category'. Will they plant fruits & vegetables? Will they grow livestock? Or will they produce a byproduct crop?"

"And I imagine that decision is informed by the type of farmer and the conditions they're working with," Casey considered.

"Correct. Now, let's see how we make the analogy to Dollar Farming. In Dollar Farming, much like traditional farming, you'll find that there are dozens of ways to have a product or service that you can bring to harvest. But ultimately, they tend to fit into a broad category, much like peaches and spinach would fall into the 'plant' category, chicken and pigs in the 'livestock' category, and eggs and milk in the 'byproduct' category. This is important because remember - the first step in 'farming' is 'choosing'. So we're looking to see what kind of income choice or 'dollar farm' a person wants to make," he said. "Let's step back and see if there are different 'broad categories' of farmed income a person might consider. Tell me about some of the different income streams we've talked about or that you and Jake explored."

"Let's see, there's rental real estate. One could also write a book. There's also the car-wash and ATM ideas you taught me about. I also learned about 'Print On Demand' as e-Commerce. That seemed like it'd fall into the 'Dollar Farming' category."

"Yes - 'Print-On-Demand' or 'POD' as it is affectionately known by some is absolutely a type of 'farmed income' - we will discuss it more specifically later," he replied. "Now, let's take a few of those examples and look a little closer to see if we can identify any 'broad categories' much like we did with traditional farming where we identified 'plant', 'livestock', and 'byproduct'."

"Ok - how do we do that?" she asked.

"When we did the same exercise for traditional farming, how did we go about it?" Elijah asked.

"I suppose we looked at what the end product was," she answered.

"Correct. We looked at the 'crop' that was brought to harvest or for sale on the market. It was either a 'plant', meat - which we called 'livestock', or a 'byproduct' which is something derived from the livestock or plants," he explained. "We could do the same to categorize the types of Dollar Farms. The best way to evaluate what category a farmed income falls under is to consider what the cultivated 'product' is that generates the revenue. In other words, what 'crop' will be harvested in step 4?" he said. "So let's think about what each of those income opportunities requires and what outcome they'll produce."

"Well, for rental real estate, you'd need a piece of property that you could convert into rental income," Casey said.

"You're on the right track," he said, "but you're being more specific than you should be. Remember - we're thinking 'broadly' here."

"Too specific, huh? Ok - this might sound dumb, but I guess for rental real estate, the 'seed' is money. You'll need money to buy the building or house that you'll be renting," she said.

"Not dumb at all. In fact - that's spot on," he said. "So in this example - it's a house or apartment unit that generates the revenue. Do you see any similarities between something like that and say, a car wash?"

She thought about it for a moment, "Not really. At least not at first. But if I think about it," Casey considered, "ultimately, it seems like it's a 'thing' that generates the revenue. Something tangible such as a rental apartment or a machine that washes cars."

"Bingo! A *thing*."

"So... 'thing' is the category?" she asked quizzically. "That seems weird."

He laughed, "I agree - 'thing' isn't really the category. But you're on the tip of it. Let me explain: in your examples, a person would purchase or build a 'thing' - or in other words, a *capital asset* that generates revenue."

"Capital asset?"

"That's right," he said. "A 'thing' of value. So in your examples, you use money to purchase 'capital' - a thing of value - that in turn generates revenue," he said. "In this farm, you have a 'capital asset' that generates your regularly recurring and predictable income."

"So the category is '*Capital*'," she realized.

He nodded. "Now, let's think of other categories. What's another type of farmed income you mentioned?"

"One of the first we discussed was writing and selling a book," she said.

"Great - and do you need capital for that? Is it a 'capital asset' in the same way that a rental property is?" he asked.

A light-bulb went on for her, "I suppose not. You wouldn't need money - other than what it'd cost to buy a laptop computer - to write a book. And the book itself isn't a 'capital asset'. So it doesn't fall under a category of 'capital'," she considered.

"So what is the 'seed' and the 'crop' you'll harvest?" Elijah nudged.

"The book is the crop," she answered.

"Hmm...yes - technically the book is what a person purchases," he said, "but isn't it really the content of the book that matters? Not so much the cover, paper, and ink but rather, how those words convey meaning?"

She thought about it some more. "You're right. So now this is gonna sound really, really dumb but the only thing I keep coming to is 'your brain'," she laughed.

"No reason to laugh, Casey and once again - not dumb at all. In fact - right on target," he agreed. "So to be a bit more technical about it, rather than your 'brain', I'd categorize this as 'intellectual property'. You have *created* something of value from your intellect that generates revenue. You own the 'intellectual property' that was a product of your *creativity*. So this farm category, as I like to describe it, is '*Creative*'."

"So we've got '*Capital*' farms, and '*Creative*' farms," she said. "I suppose that you're going to tell me that all of these categories start with the letter 'C'?"

"You know how I like to keep things structured in simple, easy-to-remember ways," Elijah said.

"I do. And candidly, I agree that it helps make things easier to remember," Casey added. "Are there any other categories?"

"There's one more broad category that I think is important to consider. Try and go back to something we spoke of just moments ago."

"Let's see," she said, "we talked about the ATM idea. But that seems like it'd fall under the 'Capital' category. It's a 'thing' you purchase with money that generates revenue."

"Very good," he exclaimed, "you're catching on quickly."

She continued, "We also just talked about Print-On-Demand - or POD as you described it. That's a type of e-Commerce. Is that one to consider?"

"Let's find out. Tell me more about what POD specifically is - to be sure we're on the same page," he requested.

"From what I understand, you set up an image, logo, or maybe just a silly saying like, 'It's Wine O'Clock,' on a web-based storefront. There are lots of web-based stores like 'Shopify', 'Etsy', or even 'Amazon'. Then, people can click and buy a product like a shirt, hat, or wine tumbler with that logo or saying imprinted on it. The company prints and ships the product to the customer and collects a fee for that while you earn a percentage of the sale," Casey explained.

"Very well said," Elijah replied. "Does that fall into what we'd define as a dollar farm?"

"I think so," Casey pondered. "You create the logo or saying once along with your internet store. Then as people buy the product, you get paid over and over. Get paid multiple times for singular work. Isn't that a Dollar Farm?"

He smiled. "I think you nailed it. So yes - it is a type of Dollar

Farm. And now, thinking about the category, what is the seed for that?" he queried.

"It seems similar to the previous example we spoke of like a book in that you're selling something that is the result of your creativity. For example, the logo or art that gets printed on the coffee mug or t-shirt comes from a creative idea," she said.

"That's true," Elijah agreed, "but people aren't so much buying the 'intellectual property' of the idea but rather the utility of the underlying product that is made more appealing because of the idea, wouldn't you agree?"

"Yeah, I suppose so," Casey answered. "There's a big difference between buying a novel that a writer poured his soul into and a T-shirt with a silly slogan printed on it."

"So go back and tell me what that industry is."

"It's called e-Commerce generically speaking," she answered. He looked at her with a knowing grin.

"Duh! 'Commerce'!" she exclaimed. "That's the category!!"

"Absolutely," Elijah replied. "The underlying harvest is simple 'Commerce' - or within the context of our dollar farm, the buying and selling of 'goods' or 'services'."

"I'm a little confused by this one, though," she said. "In some ways, it still feels like it's 'Creative' and in other ways, I feel like it's similar to the 'commissioned' salespeople we speak of as 'Dollar Hunters'. You'd earn a 'commission' each time a t-shirt or coffee mug is sold. Now I'm questioning whether this is 'farming' or 'hunting'."

"Those are both very valid points," he answered. "And in some ways, I don't entirely disagree. But there are important, critical distinctions. Let's touch upon your second point first. When we talk about 'Dollar Hunters', that is, commissioned salespeople and professionals who are paid on a 'per transaction' basis, we're typically referring to a person who earns a one-time fee for a singular transaction. To earn the next commission or fee, they have to go out and personally 'sell' it again - much like a hunter - or better yet - a fisherman who only catches a single fish with each line they drop in the water."

Casey listened intently.

He continued, "But in the e-Commerce example, like you rightly pointed out earlier, you create the work once, meaning you create the logo or slogan and make it available on the digital store. Then, each time someone buys the product, you get paid. You don't have to keep creating and placing the products yourself for each sale or transaction."

"Much like a system that might catch and retrieve multiple fish rather than a single fishing line," she added.

He agreed, "That's right. So you're correct in viewing the revenue as a commission of sorts but it gets paid over and over if you've developed a good product and system for it."

"And what about my other point? That it feels like it falls under the 'Creative' category?" she asked.

"Kudos - here you're correct in many ways. Before we come up with an answer for your thought, what were the 3 basic food farming categories we discussed?" Elijah asked.

She answered, "There were 'Plants', 'Livestock', and 'Byproducts'."

He nodded, "That third category - 'byproduct' - could it exist if it wasn't a result in some ways of 'Plants' or 'Livestock'?"

Casey smiled, "Wow! I guess not. In farming, you'd have two main categories but a third that is correlated to those two. And I guess in this example, 'Commerce' is also a 'Byproduct' category of 'Creative'."

"Or 'Capital'," he added. "The 'Commerce' category, as I

look at it, is the harvest that is likely in some ways planted in its seed with a 'Creative' idea or a 'Capital' asset."

He paused a moment before continuing, "I also want to emphasize that what you'll find is that these categories are not exact sciences. Remember, we're drawing an analogy between food farming and financial income - it will never be perfect. And many if not most of the dollar farms we discuss can be considered a 'combination' or 'hybrid' of one or more of the categories," he explained. He drew a diagram on a napkin reflecting this concept.

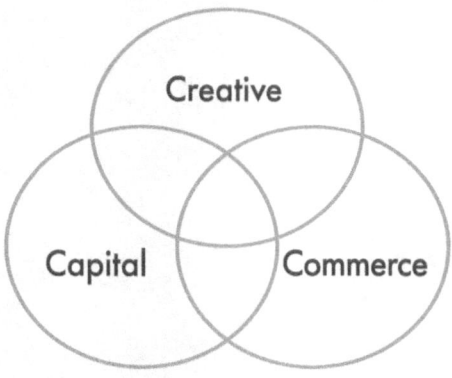

"So you are correct in saying that 'Print-On-Demand' falls into the 'Creative' category in some ways." He pointed to the spot in the diagram where "Creative" and "Commerce" overlap. "But it is primarily a part of the 'Commerce' category. As we take a deeper dive into each of these 3 categories, I hope you'll start to reflect on the aspects that make each of them unique. "After all," he continued, "the primary purpose at this juncture is to help you with Step one: 'Choosing' your Dollar Farm crop."

"Gotcha. And that's it? Those are the 3 broad categories of Dollar Farms? 'Creative', 'Capital', and 'Commerce'?" she asked.

"That's all I've got for now. I'm sure," he expanded, "that we might be able to come up with others. And that as time goes and that as technologies and industries evolve, there'll perhaps be a new category for us to add to the mix. But for now, just about every type of dollar farm is represented by one of those three categories or a combination of them."

"Just like how in food farming, most fall into either 'plants', 'livestock', or 'byproducts'," she added. "So what happens next?".

"Soon, we'll take a closer look at each one of distinct categories," he answered. "But first, we need to take a moment to reflect on *intentionality*."

## Chapter 11

# A MAP to Guide the Way

"Intentionality?" Casey remarked.

"That's right. Before we explore the 'Creative', 'Commerce', or 'Capital' groups - I want to devise a *map* for 'how' you'll look at each of those categories so that you and Jake have a comprehensive and meaningful way to decide which is the farm - or farms - you'd want to get to work on."

"What do you mean by a 'map'?" she dug.

Elijah explained, "Think about a farmer - a real farmer. They might have a plot of land to work with. Let's suppose that the land would be just as functional to grow strawberries as it would be to cultivate chickens. How would the farmer choose between those two?"

"I guess it'd be based on which would provide a better financial opportunity. Which one is most profitable," she responded.

"Fair point," he agreed. "Give me an example."

"Well," she said, "let's pretend that the farmer has done some homework and determined that a chicken farm would generate more income than planting strawberries. Then he'd deduce that it would make more financial sense to grow chickens. So he starts a chicken farm."

"But," Elijah rebutted, "what if the farmer has an aversion to animals? Or more to the point, has a passion for digging in the dirt?"

"Well, you kind of rigged the answer, didn't you?"

"Not really," Elijah said. "I'm merely trying to illustrate a fine but critical point: the financial consideration you suggested is an important one. But it can't be taken in isolation. In fact, there are 3 factors that can be considered and balanced from which a prospective dollar farmer can view or 'map' their choice of what dollar farm to cultivate. The potential profitability that you mentioned, or as I like to refer to it: the 'marketability' of a business endeavor is one of those 3. But it is not the only one and not necessarily more important than the other two."

"You mentioned in the example that maybe the farmer has a passion for 'digging in the dirt'. Is 'passion' another of the considerations?" Casey asked.

He nodded, "You are a quick student. Having a 'passion' or an intrinsic, joyful connection to a particular endeavor is another of the considerations. Remember - we started this conversation discussing 'financial freedom and *fulfillment*'. The fulfillment aspect - the idea that you will have a meaningful way to enjoy and spend your time is just as if not more important than the financial freedom that you're working towards. Having a passion for the farm you cultivate is a hugely important element in leading you towards fulfillment."

"I understand that. For example, no matter how marketable or profitable it might be, the idea of operating a car wash does absolutely nothing for me," she added. "That type of dollar farm feels like it'd be drudgery to build."

"Right! But what if you have been a car aficionado your whole life? Maybe a car wash - would speak to you."

"That makes sense. And what's the third thing? If 'marketability' and 'passion' are one and two?" she asked.

"Here's an example: What if you absolutely loved writing? You have a 'passion' for it and could spend days and days at your desk typing away. And what if we agree there's a large market for books or more specifically, the type of book you're writing? That would check off those first two boxes, right? Passion and Marketability?" he asked.

"Of course," she answered.

"But," he continued, "what if you simply didn't have talent as a writer? What if you didn't have an innate or learned *ability*? Do you think you'd find success doing it?"

She felt a bit of herself deflate like a balloon with a small puncture slowly releasing its air. "I guess not. I guess it'd be hard to turn that into a profitable dollar farm," she pondered.

"That's right. As bitter of a pill as it might be to swallow, a lack of *ability* in a critical area of a potential endeavor will almost certainly doom it to failure. For example, I have a passion for playing golf and certainly, there's a market out there for the sport. But I'm not any good at it! I'd starve to death if my income relied on it," he said.

She thought about his words a moment, then drew a diagram similar to the one he'd drawn earlier:

"So those are the three considerations you'd have us look at before starting a dollar farm: Market, Ability, and Passion,"

"Yep," he agreed. "In a perfect world, you'll choose and cultivate endeavors where you find that there is a demand or *market* for the product or service, that you have a special talent or *ability* at doing it well, and for which you feel a sense of excitement or *passion* in doing it. That recipe will not only produce the greatest chance of financial success but will also fill you with vigor and excitement."

She looked back at her diagram and noticed his clever shorthand. "Market, Ability, and Passion. I guess it's no accident that the acronym is M.A.P.," she grinned.

"No accident at all, Casey. Anytime we can make it easier to remember something, why not?" he added.

"Can we spend a few moments on each of those? Take a dive into the MAP before looking at the three farm categories - Creative, Capital, and Commerce?" she asked.

"You read my mind," Elijah answered.

## Chapter 12

# The Farmer's Market

"When we talk about 'Market', what we're really getting at is whether the product or service you're looking to harvest will have ready buyers - that is, people or organizations that have a need or desire along with an ability to pay for the harvest you are offering," Elijah said.

"I'm happy you started with 'Market'," Casey said. "I'm getting a little tripped up by the term."

"I understand," Elijah replied. "It can seem very daunting and 'business-oriented'. But I think we can simplify it so that it makes basic, common sense. Let's start by taking a look at any enterprise, no matter how large or small. Whether we're talking about a hot dog vendor in New York City's Time Square or a global behemoth like WalMart - how do those enterprises derive their income?" he posed.

"In example one, I guess it's with someone buying a hot dog. And in the case of a big company, it's with someone buying whatever it is they buy. Groceries, clothing, home goods, et cetera," Casey answered.

"That's right. How is income derived when someone lives in an apartment?" Elijah asked.

"If the person is renting, they pay rent to the landlord or whoever owns the apartment," she responded.

"And in the case of a company like yours where you work in the Marketing Department, how is revenue derived?"

She said, "Gosh - I almost forgot about my day job! I compartmentalize it when I talk to you. But our company sells household goods to other companies that then take them to the retail market. We don't sell to individuals."

"So is there a common denominator in how revenue is derived?" he asked.

She thought about it a moment then answered, "I suppose it's a matter of sales in some regard. *Something* - whether it's a product or service - is purchased by *someone*."

"*Someone* or *something*," he added. "Remember, your company doesn't sell to people, per se. It sells to other companies. But the point is the same - for an enterprise to receive revenue, it must sell something of value - most commonly a product or service - to a person or organization in exchange for money."

"So the common denominator is that every financial enterprise ultimately sells its products or services to a customer," she concluded.

"Exactly," Elijah replied. "And for there to be a customer, the product or service must have a viable market. This is an important understanding because as you begin your journey as a Dollar Farmer, you'll need to embrace the fact that you are no longer Casey and Jake, private individuals - *you are now forming an enterprise.* You'll need to recognize that *your farm is in fact a business* and as a result, you'll need to think of it that way," he finished.

"Even a book author?"

"Yes, even an author," he answered. "Dollar Farming is ultimately about getting your product or service into the hands of a paying customer. For there to be a customer, there must be a 'market' for your product. The reason I bring this up now is that we are at the stage where we 'choose' and to do so, you want to be sure you're 'choosing' a farming activity for which there is or will be a market of customers who are ready to buy."

"But I don't know how to run a business," she worried.

"You don't need to - at least not yet," Elijah replied. "The only thing you need to know for the moment is that before you choose your 'crop', you'll need to have some part of your mind directed to making sure that it will be *viable*. And for it to be viable, there must be a potential 'customer'. So I want to make sure that you are thinking 'customer' with every moment you evaluate going forward with your farm choice."

"I understand. At the end of the day, the customer is a very important element in the choice we make," she said.

"No - *the customer is the most important element*," he corrected. "Without a customer, there isn't even the possibility of a business."

"Fair enough. So for now, when I think of 'Market', what I should really be thinking is 'Customer'?" she asked.

"That's a great way to look at it," Elijah responded. "Simply ask yourself, 'Will there be potential customers for this endeavor we want to undertake? If the answer is 'no', then it probably wouldn't be worthy of consideration as a Dollar Farm."

"I understand: if there isn't someone or something that would potentially buy the product or service we are harvesting, then it isn't worth pursuing," she answered.

"It isn't worth pursuing as a dollar farm," he corrected.

"There's nothing wrong with spending time enjoying things for which you have an ability and passion. Just don't expect them to lead to 'financial freedom' via a dollar farm if there is no market for them."

"I get it. For it to be a viable dollar farm, there needs to be a customer or 'market' for it. And that helps me understand your use of the term 'Market' much better. So I don't stress about not being a business person, yet?" Casey asked.

"Please don't," he said, "in fact - we'll spend a good bit more time on the running of an enterprise - and a 'Dollar Farm' when we get to the 5th 'F' in our work together."

"My gosh!" she exclaimed. "That's right - there are 6 'F's and we're now on the 4th! So now you have me really curious. If we're talking about 'Dollar Farming' and the 4th 'F' is 'Farm', I can't even begin to imagine what 5 and 6 would be."

"You'll find out soon enough," he smiled. "Now that you have a sense of what '*Market*' is as it relates to selecting a Dollar Farm crop, let's spend a few moments on '*Passion*'."

## Chapter 13

# The Bricklayers

"If you don't mind," Elijah said, "I'd like to discuss the subject of '*Passion*' with a parable."

"Please do," she replied.

"There once was a man who walked along a dusty road. In the distance, he saw three bricklayers hard at work. When he arrived at the first of the workers, he noticed the man's expression was gruff. The traveler asked that first bricklayer, 'what are you doing?' The man replied hoarsely, 'Can't you tell? I'm laying bricks,' he snorted and got back to grudgingly placing one brick on the other."

"The traveler then walked to the second laborer whose spirits were a bit more upbeat and asked, 'what are you doing?' The second worker responded with a warm smile, 'I'm building a wall.

*That's interesting*, the traveler thought to himself. The first worker didn't make a mental correlation between the work he did or its outcome whereas the second - who seemed far happier - could see a connection between what he was doing and how it would end up.

The traveler then walked over to the third bricklayer. He noticed this worker was literally whistling as he worked and performing his service with great enthusiasm. He asked, 'what are you doing?' The third bricklayer turned with a huge, jovial smile and exclaimed, 'I'm building a house of worship for the Lord where we can gather in communion!'"

As Elijah finished the parable, Casey sat back and smiled as the lesson intuitively flowed through her. "Gosh, I never really thought about work that way," she said. "Each of the bricklayers was performing the same 'task' - doing the same work. But their internal motivation completely affected their level of enjoyment as they performed those tasks."

"Correct. The first laborer had no internal motivation - no underlying *'why'* for the duties he performed. As a result, for him it was drudgery and a chore," Elijah said. "The second worker had a small yet meaningful motivator: he was visualizing the results of his labor. He could connect the work that he did with an outcome and as a result, had a sense of enjoyment for the task at hand since he could connect it to an eventual accomplishment."

"But the third bricklayer," Casey added, "was working from a level of *inspiration*. I imagine he was a man of faith and so to him, the work he did was far more meaningful than just 'laying bricks' or even seeing the byproduct which would result in 'finishing a wall'. He could see the ultimate outcome which had meaning to him and because of that, he was actively joyful doing his work. He was *fulfilled*."

"You know, Casey, most people go through life not really thinking about things like this. There's a certain mainstream acceptance of 'work' being 'work' and not something you're necessarily supposed to enjoy. That it's a means to an end such as a 'paycheck' or access to benefits," Elijah said. "Our society has drilled the idea of '*get an education; have a career with a steady paycheck and good benefits; and save for retirement*' so deeply into us that it almost seems peculiar to question it. Of course it's no wonder that so many people sleep-walk through life on the verge of depression: they spend most of their waking hours in a job or career that brings them no fulfillment. As Thoreau said, 'Most men lead lives of quiet desperation'."

Elijah gathered himself, realizing that the topic of 'Passion' had struck a deeper chord for him and that conveying its significance to Casey mattered greatly. "I don't subscribe to that thinking," he continued, "I don't believe we are here on earth to merely exist. *I believe we are here to make a difference - to matter.* In the process, we must obviously have the financial means to live - our society demands it. But it does not demand that we do so in muted misery. So yes - your mission here is to find your passion and pursue it. And if the Dollar Farm you and Jake harvest is connected to that passion, it will be all the better," Elijah concluded.

Casey let the thought settle in her. She thought of all of the co-workers at her firm who seemed to 'sleep-walk through life' as Elijah had described it. There was Nora in finance who'd been with the firm 30 years who she'd never once seen smile. Chuck in sales who smelled of bourbon and tobacco every day. Gustavo in the logistics department whose only satisfaction seemed to arrive when he was able to berate one of his reportees on a mishandled shipment. And Lana at the reception desk who once must have harbored greater dreams than connecting inbound calls but whose dreams had likely withered in the drudgery of working 9 hour shifts for 40 hours each week the last 23 years of her life with only a 2 week yearly vacation as a reprieve.

*These are good people*, Casey thought to herself, *who have led lives of quiet desperation. That would've been me.....*

Then it struck her, "Elijah - when we first started our conversation about Dollar Farming - about finding an alternative to staying in the 'rat race', you'd mentioned that there was a danger in 'retiring'. That it increases the likelihood that a person becomes depressed. How do you reconcile that fact with what you said? That many people live lives of quiet desperation sleep-walking through their careers and life? In other words, you're suggesting we leave a career where we're subconsciously bordering on depression and yet you said that retiring increases the odds of depression. I don't understand."

Elijah nodded, "You raise a very fair point. And the answer is not a pleasant one to consider but I believe it to be true. Because most people have already subconsciously resigned themselves in some ways to a mere 'existence' rather than 'living', the 40 hour-a-week career at least provides them the bare necessities required for human satisfaction: purpose, place, and people. Even in the least satisfying of careers, most workers are at least able to find some measure of those 3 things, without which, life really does become drudgery. In other words, try and imagine a life where you don't have a 'reason to wake up in the morning', a place you're needed, or people to spend time with. That would be truly depressing for most people. So at a minimum, a dull, uninspired job provides at least those elements," he countered. "And consequently, that is why retirement for many people ends up being even more depressing than the career they retired from. That is why all of this is connected to that first 'F' we discussed: *'Fulfillment'*. Remember, you are working towards financial freedom *and* fulfillment. So my thought is to implore people to do otherwise - to lead with passion and build a life both in work and play that is connected to things that inspire and excite you."

"So how do I find that?" Casey asked. "How do I discover the thing that makes me 'passionate' and connect it to my Dollar Farm?"

"It needn't be too complicated," he answered. "I don't want you to mistake my use of the word 'passion' with an overt expectation that you must be engaged at hyper-visceral levels to every thing you do each waking moment. I'm merely suggesting that when possible, your pursuits and endeavors be connected to things you care about. Things that carry meaning for you. Go back to our lesson on 'fulfillment' and think about the things that got you excited or energized then."

"I can completely appreciate that, Elijah. But it's hard for me to consider anyone having a 'passion' or even basic 'excitement' over an ATM business. Or selling coffee mugs on the internet," Casey retorted. "I don't mean to sound cynical but must everything we do have 'passion' or 'purpose' or even 'excitement' behind it for it to be a viable Dollar Farm? I know you can't have a Dollar Farm without there being a 'Market' - we learned that just now. But can you have a Dollar Farm if you don't have 'Passion' for the thing you're building?"

He nodded, "You're right. Not every endeavor will be exciting. Or even 'interesting' by traditional standards. Not every opportunity will have 'passion' attached to it and that doesn't alone make it unworthy to consider. But in a world that has become so disconnected from purpose and meaning, I'm trying to make sure that it remains part of the conversation - an important part. And that we as individuals collectively strive towards building lives that have meaning. So to the extent that any professional opportunity you pursue gives you a chance to do something you find fulfillment or excitement in - whether it be in the harvesting of income on a dollar farm you build - or even just in a good, old nine-to-five job - you should gravitate towards that. Because it will make the work itself seem a lot less like work and a lot more like inspiration."

"Like the bricklayer building a house of worship he was passionate about," Casey recalled from the parable.

"Exactly right," answered Elijah.

## Chapter 14

# The Difference between 'Willing' and 'Able'

"The last of the considerations," Elijah said, "is 'Ability'."

"In other words, if I'm not good at something, I probably won't be very successful turning it into a profitable Dollar Farm," Casey added.

"In a nutshell, yes," he answered. "You must have some proficiency to have success in any opportunity you pursue. But there are 2 key areas here that are easily overlooked."

"What are those?" she asked.

Elijah answered, "Firstly, you'd want to identify the areas of talent or ability you'd need for a particular endeavor. For example, if we think about someone who wants to pursue writing books as a Dollar Farm, it's easy to recognize that you have to have an 'ability' as a writer. But what is the talent or ability you'd need if you wanted to become a landlord who rents apartment units?"

"I guess you'd need to be good at buying and renting properties," she answered.

"Generally speaking, yes. But the key talent in this example is *knowing which properties and at what price*," he replied. "In other words, it isn't good enough to purchase a random apartment building or house and put it up for rent. You'd need to know which property would be the easiest and most cost-effective to bring to the market. That is a talent."

"So does every endeavor have its own unique talents or abilities that are required?" she asked.

"I believe so," Elijah said. "Some are simply more obvious than others to identify. Knowing that to be an author, you'd need a talent for writing or to be a photographer, you'd need a talent for picture-taking is a far more easily recognizable ability than knowing what talent is required for building an online t-shirt selling business or becoming an ATM operator. But that doesn't mean that those don't have barriers to entry that don't include a talent or ability."

"The key is in being able to identify them and then reflect back upon yourself: 'do I have the talent or ability for that?'" she added.

"That's right. Which then leads to my second point regarding 'ability'," Elijah said. "Not all talents or abilities need to be 'innate'. Many can be learned and developed. You don't have to necessarily be 'born with it'."

"So even if I don't have a developed ability for a particular endeavor, I might be able to learn it," she added.

"Exactly. When I gave the earlier example of a would-be writer who had a passion and for whom there was a viable market but who didn't have the talent, it doesn't mean they can't pursue that endeavor. It just means that they need to be willing to develop the skill before they expect it to be successful and profitable," Elijah said. "Most people aren't born out of the womb with any of the talents they'll need to be successful in any particular endeavor.

Sure - some have certain innate abilities or gifts and the degree to which you can rely on any of those is fantastic. But I wouldn't want you to be discouraged from pursuing an endeavor just because you don't already have the skills required. You'd just have to be honest with yourself in knowing what skill you'd need for a respective endeavor and then have the willingness to develop that skill."

"That's reassuring," Casey said. "I was a bit concerned that I might choose a Dollar Farm that I lacked the necessary ability required. But knowing that I might be able to develop that ability over time makes me feel better."

"I'd like to add something else to the conversation about 'Ability'," Elijah said. "While it makes sense to consider the abilities or talents that are required from a certain financial opportunity, and then see if you have them or are able to develop them, there is another angle."

"What angle?" she asked.

He replied, "Start by looking at yourself in the mirror. Ask yourself, 'what special talents or abilities do I already have?' Then, see if you can match those abilities with a marketable business opportunity that can generate recurring revenue."

"That makes a lot of sense!" Casey exclaimed. "For example, I know I'm a good marketer - it's the field I'm already in. So I'd look to see what Dollar Farms might benefit from that talent."

"Bingo. And lucky for you, in some regards, marketing is helpful for any of the endeavors you'll consider. After all, in some regards, each of these is a 'business' or 'enterprise'. I would encourage you to think of other things you or Jake are already good at. Then see how you might apply them to an opportunity."

"That's exciting - and empowering," Casey smiled. "I can think about things I'm good at and see if they are in industries that get me excited or energized."

"Exactly," he answered. "So now you have a frame - or better yet, a *MAP* that will help you determine what opportunity you and Jake might want to pursue."

"Is there a certain way we should go through that? When using the *MAP* technique?" she asked.

"Yes - one way is you'd ponder the prospective opportunity in that order: Market, Ability, and Passion or MAP for short. I'd start with the basic question: 'Is there a market for this?'" Elijah said.

"Because if there isn't, there is no viable 'Dollar Farm'," she added.

"That's right," he said, "and in many regards, the '3 C's' we identified earlier - 'Creative', 'Capital', and 'Commerce' - on which we are about to spend a bit more time on are already identified as viable 'markets'. We'll have done some of that work already. So once we've picked a few opportunities that pique your interest, then you can move on to the next area: *Ability*. Ask yourself: what skills, talents, or abilities will this particular opportunity require? Do I have those abilities? If not, am I willing to do the work to learn and develop them?"

"And if I'm not willing to develop those necessary skills," she started.

"Then it's not a Dollar Farm for you," he finished.

"Right. Then lastly, if I have or am willing to develop the necessary skills, I should see if it's something for which I find passion or energy," Casey surmised. "Like the 3rd bricklayer who connected his work with something he cared deeply about - building a house of worship."

"And in all likelihood, if it was something that piqued your interest in the first place, it likely already does," he indicated. "If, on the other hand, it doesn't seem to resonate from a place of 'passion', you'll want to at least view it from the same perspective as the 2nd bricklayer. Make an association of the work you'd be doing harvesting this dollar farm with an outcome: the financial freedom you seek and the other ways you'll find 'fulfillment'."

"That makes a lot of sense," she said. "And I suppose the other way would be to do what you described: see if there's something I have a talent or ability for and then see if there's a market for it."

"Correct," he answered. "So instead of MAP, it'd be AMP!"

Casey sensed herself starting to bubble with giddiness. "Ok - I'm ready."

"Yes," Elijah smiled, "Our next step is to take a closer look at each one of the 'Dollar Farming' categories."

Chapter 15

# The Artistpreneur

The next week, Casey and Elijah met at their city's performing arts center. They sat in the cavernous orchestral hall where symphonies, ballets, plays, operas, and musicals are performed. Casey admired the beauty of the hall - its design seemed to serve both its form and its function. The house of the theater was filled with lush, red velvet chairs, while the sides held ornate balcony boxes. The stage proscenium arch and apron were adorned with carved swirls and inlaid flowers made of painted wood and mother of pearl. Casey imagined the house filled with enthusiastic patrons enjoying a performance on the stage.

"This is beautiful," she remarked. "I can't believe Jake and I haven't come yet."

"My family and I have enjoyed the wonderful performances here for many years. I'm sure you and Jake would too," Elijah said. He then pivoted to the conversation at hand, "Tell me Casey, can you imagine why I'd bring you here to discuss Dollar Farming?"

Casey thought about it for a moment, "I know we're ready to take a deeper dive into the three Dollar Farm categories, so

I'm guessing it has to do something with one of those categories, though I can't think of what it would be just yet."

"Let's start this way. Earlier, we agreed that there were 3 basic categories of Dollar Farms: 'Creative', 'Capital', and 'Commerce'," Elijah said. "Each one has unique characteristics and specific 'types' of businesses or 'farms' that fall into them. But all of these categories have one thing in common: they pay regularly recurring revenue."

"Do the hard work once, and have it pay you over and over and over," Casey added.

"Correct," he agreed. "An author writes a book that pays a royalty each time someone buys it. A landlord collects rent each month from the tenant that lives in his apartment. An online website store gets paid every time someone buys their logoed coffee mug."

"But the underlying crop," she added, "the product or service that generates that income has a different dynamic depending on whether it is primarily 'Creative', 'Capital', or 'Commerce'. Is that right?"

Elijah smiled, "Exactly."

"So we're here in a performing arts center where symphonies and musicals would be performed. A place where 'art' comes to life," she said. "When I think of art, I think of creativity. Is that the first type of Farm we'll be discussing? The 'Creative' type?"

He nodded, "That's right. The 'Creative' category of 'Dollar Farms' is in many ways, the most intriguing to me," Elijah started. "Just a generation ago, many of the Farms in this category would have been out of reach for the kinds of farmers that might seek to till them. But now, creatives can find an opportunity to find financial freedom and fulfillment. It holds much promise for those 'farmers' who don't have very much - if any money with which to start their farms. That's because typically, the only investment required is that of your creativity, time, and tenacity."

Casey listened intently as Elijah continued, "And for many of the 'crops' in the 'Creative' category, there are truly no barriers to entry. So let's discuss what some of the key characteristics are that define a 'Creative' Dollar Farm. What comes to mind for you?"

Casey pondered it for a moment, "My impression is that a 'Creative' Dollar Farm is one where the 'crop' is really an 'idea' or the product of creative 'thinking'."

Elijah challenged her, "But don't all businesses start with an 'idea'?"

"Yes," Casey answered, "but in a 'Creative' Dollar Farm, the 'idea' itself is the product. It's what the customer is buying."

"I don't understand," he rebutted, "how does a person *buy an idea*? Ideas aren't 'things' - they're intangible."

"That's true - the idea or creative thoughts have to be turned into a tangible item or service. But the tangible product isn't the thing of value - it's the idea it contains," she said.

Elijah smiled, "Very good. So for a person to be a 'Creative Dollar Farmer', the crop they are selling is in fact their *intellectual property* - their 'creation', so-to-speak."

Casey nodded, "I think that's right."

"So can you give me an example or two of what that might mean?" he asked.

She looked around at the concert hall where they sat before answering, "Well, I imagine a composer's symphony is their 'creation'. A playwright or for that matter, the writer of a musical is also 'creating' something."

"Those are good examples," Elijah acknowledged. "I see you're drawing your inspiration from our beautiful surroundings. One of the things I enjoy most about this space is that it harkens back to an era long before the digital, on-demand world we now live in."

Casey agreed, "You're right. I can even picture couples getting dressed for a 'night out at the theater,' and arriving by horse and buggy to enjoy a performance of Tchaikovsky's 'Swan Lake'. But I'm not sure how those 'creations' I just mentioned could ever be Dollar Farms."

"Tell me," Elijah asked, "what are some of the fundamental differences between how you might have 'experienced art' in the horse and buggy days compared to now?"

She thought about it a moment, then said, "For starters, if I wanted to listen to a symphony back then, I guess you'd have to actually, physically come to a theater."

"And now?" he asked.

"I can pull up *Spotify* or *Apple Music* and stream just about any song or musical recording I'd ever want to listen to. Same thing with a ballet like 'Swan Lake'. I'm sure I could find a recorded performance that I could watch - maybe on *YouTube* or a streaming service."

"Good," Elijah replied. "Let's keep exploring this line of thinking. What are some of the other 'art forms' that come to mind? Not necessarily those that'd be performed here but just in general."

"Well, we've talked about books before," Casey answered. "In the past, you'd have to get your books from a store or library. Now, they can just be delivered straight to your door."

"That's right - and how else might you access books? In ways that didn't exist 30 or even 15 years ago?"

"Now, I can read them on an e-reader like a 'Kindle' or my tablet," she answered. "And I can even 'listen' to books on audio."

He nodded. "Good - what about other art forms? Or creative endeavors?"

"Hmm," she thought. "How about movies? I suppose that once upon a time, the only way to see a movie was to go to an actual theater," she said. "Now, movie theaters themselves are struggling to stay afloat since people watch movies and shows from the comforts of their homes or wherever they are. People watch movies and all kinds of video content on their phones, tablets, or laptops."

"Exactly right," he said. "So the way we can 'experience' art in all its forms has radically changed in the last few decades."

"I agree," she nodded, "but I'm still not sure how that translates to a 'Creative' Dollar Farm, Elijah. Isn't the *Dollar Farmer* in this equation the person that is 'creating' and in some regards, 'selling' their creation? The author of the book, the songwriter, and the filmmaker? But you're talking about us - the customers - who are enjoying the art."

Elijah smiled, "Absolutely. So let's explore that. First and foremost, here's a truth that is universal to all Dollar Farms, whether we're talking about a 'Creative' farm or one of the other categories: the revenue that the farmer receives is based on an exchange of money for a product or service. We agreed that on the 'Creative' farms, the product or service is the 'Creation' such as the book, song, film, or any other type of 'intellectual property' that is purchased and consumed by the customer."

He then asked, "How does the fact that all of these types of 'Creations' are easier for a customer to access benefit the creator?"

"Putting it that way, I realize that it expands the market that any artistic or creative person can sell their work in. In a way, most 'creations' are accessible just about anywhere in the world," Casey summarized.

"Correct," Elijah exclaimed. "Whether you're a photographer, filmmaker, author, blogger, teacher, or composer, your ability to share your art, idea, or creation has greatly expanded in the last few decades simply because of technology and the wonders of a globally connected world."

He leaned in, "But let's pivot away from the customer and now towards the creator. Because advancements in technology have completely eviscerated the traditional barriers of entry for most creative people."

"How so?" she asked.

"Let's consider a few examples: an author, a songwriter, and a filmmaker," Elijah said. "Starting with an author, tell me how you envision them getting their book to the market."

"Hmm," Casey pondered, "I suppose they have to find a publisher - a company that would be willing to read their book, decide to print it, and get it out to the buying public."

Elijah smiled, "Not too long ago, that would have been the right answer for just about every author. An aspiring writer had to work hard in hopes of having a big publishing company decide to take a chance on an unknown author and get their books into stores. And since it was a difficult and expensive proposition for a publishing company to bring a new author to the market, publishers were very selective about who they'd take a chance on."

"So an aspiring writer had a very small chance of getting their books to the market," Casey concluded.

"Correct," he said. "But let's go back to what you'd mentioned when discussing the different ways you can now buy or access a book. You said that in addition to bookstores, you can buy a book online, read it on a tablet, or listen to an audio version of it. In fact, more books are now bought online than in bookstores."

"It's easier to 'buy' a book - I get that," Casey responded. "But I still don't understand how that helps a writer 'sell' a book. To bring a book to the market."

"If a book doesn't have to sit in a bookstore - or actually - if thousands of books don't have to sit in bookstores waiting to be bought, then where do the books exist prior to being bought?" Elijah asked.

"You mean the ones that are bought online from a place like Amazon?" she asked.

He nodded.

"I suppose in an Amazon warehouse somewhere," she answered.

Elijah smiled and shook his head slowly. "What if I told you that not a single copy of a writer's book needs to physically sit anywhere before you decide to buy it from Amazon?"

"Then where is the book?" she asked.

Elijah smiled, "Where is any digital information stored? Until it needs to become a physical copy?"

"You mean, it just lives in a computer server somewhere? And then the book is printed specifically for me when I buy it?" she asked.

He nodded, "Yes - it is 'printed-on-demand'."

Casey's face lit up as the revelation dawned on her, "So let me see if I follow this. Since there is no need to print, warehouse, and pre-sell thousands of books to bookstores, there is virtually no cost associated with 'making a book', at least not until it's actually printed and shipped to the customer."

"And even less of a cost to have it downloaded onto an e-reader," he added. "As a matter of fact, this is what we'll call *distribution of goods* and the degree to which it has been almost entirely digitized has revolutionized both the 'Creative' Dollar Farms as well as the type of Dollar Farm we'll discuss next."

"Wow. So how does that affect the aspiring writers we were talking about?" she asked.

"If there is virtually no cost to have a book published, what do you think that means to 'publishing' and more specifically, to the need of having a 'publisher'?"

She thought about it, then said, "This might sound weird but I suppose that it eliminates the need for a publisher."

"That's not weird at all," Elijah commented. "In fact, it's exactly right. A writer can now 'self-publish' and not be restricted by whether or not a traditional publisher chooses to buy their book."

"So if I understand correctly," Casey considered, "being a 'published author' in the past allowed that person to be a 'Dollar Farmer'. But the difference is that it was much, *much* more difficult to become a 'published author' in the past."

Elijah agreed, "Yep. Authors who in the past - and even presently - worked with traditional publishers have Dollar Farms of their own. But the new era allows *anybody* to be a published author. Furthermore, the financial calculation has also changed because in the traditional model, the publisher kept the over-whelming majority of royalties whereas now, the author keeps most of the royalties."

"That's so interesting. It really is a great, new world of opportunity for would-be authors," Casey said. "And there are self-published authors who are making an actual living doing this?"

"Of course," he answered. "I'm not saying it's easy to become a *successful* self-published author. Nothing worthwhile is ever easy. But do you remember when we started our discussions? I mentioned that there was an author who had 5 books that each sold about 1000 copies each month."

"I do remember," she said. "I think you said the math worked out to about $5 of royalties per copy sold." Casey thought back to their conversation. "That's $25,000 of income each month."

Elijah smiled.

"When you first shared that example, I really didn't understand how it was possible," Casey said. "But now I see it. I get it."

"Good. Authors - writing a book, that's just one example of one Dollar Farm in the Creative sphere. But there are so many. So let's continue this exploration," Elijah said. "Let's pivot to another 'creative' type."

"Ok," she said. "You'd mentioned people who write music. How can that be a Dollar Farm?" she asked.

"Great. Let's talk about songwriters and musicians. How has the business and market landscape changed for them, do you think?" Elijah asked.

"I have to imagine it is a similar story for musicians as it is for authors," she considered. "Starting with how I listen to music now: I can stream it straight from my phone or computer. I don't physically have to buy a CD, cassette, or vinyl - though my fiance Jake has an awesome record collection!"

"Truly, there really isn't anything quite like the feel of the needle coming down to play a 12 inch record on a turntable," he said nostalgically. "But to your point, in the same sense that the way that books are 'distributed' has changed, so has the way music is distributed."

"What you'd mentioned earlier. *'The distribution of goods'*," she said.

"Good. I'm glad you have already started thinking about that."

"So in the past," Casey said, "someone had to buy a 'thing' that had the music on it. Like a CD, cassette, or record. And I'm guessing that there were companies that served the same 'middle-man' purpose to musical artists that publishing houses served to writers before they could 'self-publish'."

"Correct. Those are called record labels," Elijah added.

Casey smiled to herself, "I remember my uncle telling me about how he was in a rock band in New York City when he was in college. He said they would gig at clubs and bars hoping they'd get 'signed' by a label. I guess that's what you mean."

"In the past, an artist's only hope of selling their music broadly was for a record label to sign them to a contract. A 'record deal'. But like publishing houses for authors, because the record label fronted most of the expenses associated with recording the music in a professional studio, having the vinyls, cassettes, and CDs made, distributing those products to record stores, and then marketing the artist, the record labels ultimately kept most of the revenue from the sales of those albums," he answered.

"But now, since the music can go straight onto a digital server - similar to how a book does until it is 'printed on demand' - there's no need for a record label to make all those physical copies of the music. And because it's streamed without need for a CD or vinyl, there's no need for a record label," Casey answered.

"Especially when you consider that most artists can record professional quality material on their home laptop computers," he said. "So while record labels still exist - just like publishing houses still exist - they simply aren't necessary anymore for an aspiring songwriter or musical artist to record and release their music to the world."

"I've heard you use the terms 'songwriter' and 'musical artist' at different times. Is there a difference?" Casey asked.

"Sure," Elijah nodded. "Think of the songwriter as the person who actually writes the songs and the artist as the one that performs them. Often, those might be one and the same but sometimes, they are different people. For example, Taylor Swift is acclaimed for both her songwriting and her performance ability. Beyonce often co-writes her songs with other writers who'll never see the stage. And the musical landscape offers recurring revenue opportunities for both writers and performers."

"So a person might be a great writer but a lousy singer or performer," Casey said. "And someone else might be wonderful behind a microphone or on stage, but not able to write a good song by themselves. But both have opportunities to create a 'Dollar Farm'?"

"Absolutely - there are royalties that pay both types of creators. And if you have the good fortune of both being a good writer *and* performer, you'll earn both types of royalties," he said.

"I guess my uncle was born at the wrong time in history!" she said. "He was writing music at a time when you needed to get 'signed' to a record deal. But now, all of that has changed."

"In some ways," Elijah answered. "But remember, if he's a good songwriter, there are opportunities for him now in this new world. There's nothing that stops him - whatever his age - from recording the songs he wrote and releasing them through the streaming platforms like Spotify. In fact, his only limitation might be those pre-conceived ideas that he's told himself. Like, 'I'm too old'," Elijah sneered, "Nonsense."

Casey sat back and thought about it a moment. "I remember when we spoke earlier about it 'never being too late'. That anyone at any age can become a 'Dollar Farmer'. I didn't really appreciate what you meant. But I'm starting to see how that's true. My uncle *could* record and release his songs. A retiree *could* write and 'self-publish' a book that goes on to be successful. And I imagine many of the other Farms we'll discuss aren't limited by a person's age."

He smiled, "The only barriers to entry are the limitations we place on ourselves. *We live in an age where anyone at any age can become a Dollar Farmer and achieve financial freedom and fulfillment.*"

"I'm going to speak to my uncle. He may have a 'Dollar Farm' that he hasn't even considered," she said. "Can a songwriter really record their music at home on their computer? Will it be good enough?"

"Absolutely. I'll give you a perfect example," Elijah answered, "Billie Eilish and her brother Finneas O'Connell wrote and recorded her entire Grammy winning album *When We All Fall Asleep, Where Do We Go?* in his bedroom."

"That's unbelievable," she remarked. Casey sat back, then asked, "What about filmmaking?" Casey asked. "We started by pondering authors and songwriters but you mentioned that we'd also discuss filmmaking. Can *anyone* really be a filmmaker? And create a Dollar Farm? That doesn't seem possible!"

"Absolutely! In many ways, this is the most accessible Creative Dollar Farm. But it will also require a more open-minded approach. This may feel a bit further out of reach for some people at first glance. But if you are willing to think about it with an open mind," Elijah said, "then I think you'll come to agree that yes, anyone can be a filmmaker and that the opportunities to create a Dollar Farm as a filmmaker are even more accessible than they are for authors and songwriters."

"Ok - I'm willing to see where this goes," she said. "But I have to admit that I'm a bit skeptical here."

"I completely understand, Casey," Elijah replied. "I'll be the first to admit that if the word 'filmmaking' conjures images of superheroes and action movies with lots of explosions and special effects, then you're probably right. Most people aren't in a position to finance and create that kind of 'film' on their own."

She added, "And if they are, they probably are financially well past the point that they'd want to create a Dollar Farm."

"Touché," he laughed. "But let's be a bit more flexible with our terms. Earlier, we looked at how musicians can now record professional music from the comfort of their own homes. The types of advances made in digital computing that make home recording possible also exist in the realm of movie making. After all, the camera on the back of your phone is in many regards higher quality than traditional cameras from just a few decades ago that used actual film."

"Interesting," she said.

"What are some of the ways you can think of that people already use their phone cameras to share experiences and ideas with others?" he asked.

"I suppose by sharing experiences on social media like Facebook, Instagram, and TikTok," Casey answered. "But that's not 'filmmaking'."

"Why not?" he asked.

"I don't know. I guess I don't think of a teenager posting a 15 second video as a 'film'," she answered.

"They may not rise to the level of a Martin Scorsese, Jordan Peele, or Greta Gerwig film," Elijah replied, "but ultimately, what we're talking about when we drill down to the most basic common denominator, is 'audio / visual entertainment'. And from my perspective - for our purposes - that's what 'filmmaking' is."

"Hmm. That's an interesting way of looking at it. But is it a Dollar Farm? Do kids make money from social media apps?" she asked.

"There are programs on social media that pay the creators of those videos if they get enough views," he said. "But I want you to consider a site that really is geared towards allowing video creators to upload longer videos. Videos of any kind. It's a site that has billions of active users."

"Of course," Casey smiled, "YouTube. Everyone watches YouTube."

"That's right," Elijah agreed. "YouTube has done for 'filmmaking' what Amazon did for book sales and sites like

Spotify and Apple Music did for music distribution."

"So you're saying," she said, "that *anyone* can upload their videos to YouTube and as a result, be a Dollar Farmer."

"Correct, Casey," he nodded. "*Anyone* can in fact be a filmmaker."

"But how does that translate into revenue?" she asked. "I completely understand that when an author sells a book on Amazon, they get paid for the book sale. And when someone streams a song or album on Spotify, the songwriter and performer can also earn a royalty. But I don't pay to watch videos on YouTube. How does the person who uploaded that earn any money?"

"That's a great observation," Elijah said. "Firstly, some people do pay by having a premium YouTube subscription. But for those that don't, there still exists a revenue model that qualifies it as a 'Dollar Farm' for the creators. When you watch a video on YouTube, what typically precedes the video?"

She thought about it a moment, "An advertisement. There's almost always an ad."

"That's right," he added, "And that means a company paid money to have their ad roll before, and in some cases, during the video. The advertising money is divided - some stays with YouTube and the rest goes to the video creator."

"Make a video once, get paid every time it gets watched," she smiled.

"The textbook definition of a Dollar Farm," he nodded.

"I guess I wouldn't have thought of this as 'filmmaking' but now I see how a person can make and upload videos to YouTube and create a revenue stream for themselves." Casey sat back and smiled.

She said, "You know, when you first mentioned people using their phone cameras to share videos, I thought to myself, 'who would want to watch my home videos'? But I realize when I go on YouTube, I see so many different kinds of videos. 'How-To' videos, travel videos, entertaining and funny videos. Videos of interviews on topics of interest. Educational videos. I even play videos of fish with cheesy New Age music to keep my cats entertained while Jake and I go to work," she laughed.

She reflected on the thought for a moment, then asked, "Do you mean to tell me that the person that uploaded that fish video is making money while we're at work? Even though there's no person in the video and no person speaking? The YouTuber that uploaded that video is making money while my cats watch fish swim on a screen?"

Elijah smiled and nodded.

"Wow!" she exclaimed. "Yeah, this is a world I'd not even realized existed, Elijah."

"And I'm happy you brought those videos up," he said. "For one thing, it shows that in what I'm describing as 'filmmaking', there's all kinds of videos that creative people can make. Travel videos, funny videos, 'how-to' videos and yes, even videos to entertain your cats!"

They laughed together. He continued, "And that kind of diverse opportunity exists in all of these kinds of Dollar Farms we've discussed. An aspiring author doesn't have to try and be the next Stephen King or Margaret Atwood."

"Margaret Atwood? She wrote *The Handmaid's Tale* - my favorite book!" Casey exclaimed.

"That's right," Elijah continued, "Someone might be a fantastic writer of fiction. And they can pursue that by self-publishing their novel. But if that's not their strength, the same opportunities exist for writers of 'Self-Help' books or 'How-To' books. Just like they do for people who make and upload videos on YouTube."

"And I'm guessing that creatives in the music space also have similar opportunities that range across a spectrum," Casey said. "Sure, you can be a rap artist or pop music writer. But maybe a songwriter that specializes in a different genre can still find options out there."

"Of course. And take it a step further," Elijah said, "they can take their talent to a different medium. For example, creating 'cheesy New Age music' that someone might post for a fish video on YouTube is another example of how a music creative can have their music 'licensed' and be paid for it."

"Oh my gosh," she said as her thoughts circled back to the YouTube video she plays for her cats. "You're right. There's music in everything. Movies, TV shows, video games."

"Ways that simply didn't exist a mere 10 or 15 years ago. The key is to be open-minded and understand as a Dollar Farmer to…"

"*To stop trading your time for Dollars*," she interrupted. "To stop being a Dollar Hunter or a Dollar Gatherer and build Dollar Farms that pay recurring revenue."

"That's right," he smiled.

"And I imagine these kinds of opportunities now extend to all types of creative fields like photographers and painters," she said.

"Absolutely," Elijah answered. "In fact, my wife Rebecca is a painter who has established her own Dollar Farms."

"Really?" Casey exclaimed. "What kind of Dollar Farm does she have?"

"We'll talk about Rebecca's farms soon. But what I'm hoping to emphasize is how creative people from all backgrounds and disciplines now have not just an opportunity to bring their creativity to markets around the world but also be able to turn that creativity into recurring revenue streams. "

Casey looked back at the stage and admired the live performances that took place there. And at the same, she recognized how much the world had changed and as a result, the opportunities that now existed for creative people to find financial freedom and fulfillment. She smiled to herself.

Elijah said, "You know, I brought you here - to a performing arts center - because I thought it would serve as a good springboard to discuss 'creative' types like traditional artists along with the ways in which the world has changed that now makes it possible for those types of creators to build Dollar Farms for themselves."

"I completely understand," Casey nodded.

## Chapter 16

# The Artist Formerly Known As....

"Having said that, there are a few other types of Dollar Farms that I believe belong in the 'Creative' category but don't exactly fit the 'artist' type we've been discussing. In some regards, they might be even more accessible to more potential Dollar Farmers than the artistic ones we've just gone through," he said. "And to take it one step further, from my view, they share several characteristics with the next type of Dollar Farm we'll be discussing."

"Cool - I'd love to learn more," she answered.

"Earlier, we spoke of ways you can access music," Elijah said.

"Do you mean by streaming on services like Apple Music and Spotify?" Casey asked.

He nodded, "That's right. But aside from music, what else can you listen to on services like those?"

"Hmm," she pondered, "come to think of it, I listen to a lot of podcasts. Maybe even more than music."

"Podcasts have become a favorite among listeners. In fact, many people even *watch* podcasts on video streaming services," Elijah said.

"I never thought of them as income generating but...why not?" He agreed, "Well curated, successful podcasts can earn meaningful revenue for their creators and hosts. One of the ways is through advertising dollars. Either through direct sponsorship or passive advertising."

"I actually listen to a podcast that offers a 'premium' service to paid subscribers. I imagine that's another way that a podcast can generate passive income," Casey added.

"Absolutely," Elijah said. "What types of podcasts do you listen to?"

"I am a big fan of true-crime stories. I find the psychology behind them so fascinating," she answered. "I also like 'advice' podcasts and 'conversational' podcasts. Where a host or panel talks about topics of interest. And Jake is into tinkering with gadgets. Like repairing old motorcycle engines. Believe it or not, there are podcasts about stuff like that."

"Great - as with all types of farms, there's a great variety of styles," he said, "which means that for a prospective Dollar Farmer interested in starting a podcast, there might be a topic that would be interesting for them to work on."

"And I suspect they might explore those interests using the MAP method," she added.

"Correct," he replied. "And in mentioning those types of podcasts, it helps point to another type of 'Creative' Dollar Farm we can consider."

"How so?" she asked.

"If someone listens to podcasts because they have an interest in learning more about something, what are other things they might do to learn more about the subject?" Elijah asked her.

"There's always books and videos," she answered, "but we've talked about those."

"That's true - and those are great Dollar Farms, as we've discussed," he replied. "But traditionally, how do you gain expertise in a topic? Any topic?"

She sat back and pondered it before answering, "You go to school. You take classes."

"Perfect," he acknowledged. "And once upon a time, you had to *physically* go to school to take a class. But hasn't that changed dramatically in many of the same ways that writing and music industries have changed?"

"Absolutely! I can take classes virtually," she answered. "So in this case, wouldn't the 'Dollar Farmer' be the teacher? But if I'm teaching a class virtually, how is that a recurring income stream? I'd be tied to teaching the class."

"That'd be true if you were teaching the class *live*," he said. "But why couldn't you create a class including a lecture, presentation, and downloadable materials for your students. In that way, students take the class at their convenience and go at their own pace."

"Of course! In fact, that's how Jake does all of his Continuing Education classes as an attorney," she remarked.

"And the spectrum of classes for people who want to learn more and are willing to pay a price for their education is growing by the day," he added. "For example, earlier I'd mentioned that my wife is an artist with a Dollar Farm of her own. One of the things she's done is create a series of online classes that artists and hobbyists pay for to improve their skills as painters."

"That's so cool," Casey said. "Create the class once, get paid over and over."

He nodded, "Think about it - just about everyone has something that they have expertise in. Especially those with life experience. So, many of us have something we could teach that could be converted into a class that someone else would be willing to pay for. Whether it's personal finance, painting, computer programming, graphic design…anything. You could create a course on marketing, for example."

"And where does somebody find a course like that?" she asked.

"There are sites that are specifically created to deliver online education. Sites like Udemy or Skillshare. There, an educator posts their courses for a price. A percentage of that payment would go to the sponsor site and the rest is paid out to the creator of the class," he explained.

"I've heard of those," Casey acknowledged. "It never occurred to me that the creator of the class was getting paid 'over and over'."

He nodded, "Another way - which is what my wife does - is to have your own website where the students pay for and access the course directly."

Casey sat back, enthralled at all the new possibilities swirling in her head. "The possibilities seem endless," she said.

"They really are, Casey. But like we'd said at the outset - this all starts with a *shift in thinking*. If you are willing to look at the world through a lens of recurring revenue - of Farming for Dollars instead of Hunting or Gathering them, all sorts of possibilities will begin to reveal themselves to you. Hundreds and hundreds of opportunities that we haven't even begun to touch upon."

"But as we explore the other types of farms - the 'Commerce' and 'Capital' ones, we will touch upon them, correct?" she queried.

"We'll go over many - especially those that are obvious and that help paint the picture for the category of Farm we're discussing," he answered. "But it's impossible to go over all of them. Remember, even as we speak, there are new types of Farms that are being created by savvy people who are shifting the economic landscape and becoming Farmers instead of Gatherers. You can be one of those."

Casey smiled as she pondered the many possibilities - both the ones they'd discussed and the many they'd never even get to in the course of their conversation.

## Chapter 17

# Reel World Imagination

That next week, Casey plunged herself headfirst into an ocean of new thinking. As she scrolled on her computer through page after page of the Kindle book 'best-sellers' list seeing otherwise unknown authors achieve phenomenal success, she appreciated one of the first lessons she'd learned from Elijah - that the way of the Dollar Farmer starts with a 'Choice': to not accept the traditional view of trading 'hours' for 'dollars'. That a singular effort can pay income multiple times and that the barriers to entry have been reduced or eliminated. Here, she saw writers who may have never had an opportunity with a traditional publisher now have books that were selling tens of thousands of copies. She dug deeper and saw songwriters who'd once lived at the mercy of the whims of a record label now bring their craft to the world. And creators - crafts people, intellectuals, artists, travelers, and comedians posting all kinds of videos on YouTube. *And getting paid.*

Casey couldn't see herself as a romance novelist or a mystery writer. She didn't know how to write or sing a song. And she wasn't sure she could make a video that anyone would want to watch.

But she could see herself as *someone* who could do *something* and for the moment, that was enough.

*I can be a Dollar Farmer. I can be financially free. I can enjoy my time as I choose. My life can be my own.*

She examined the world around her seeking 'Creative' ways to earn recurring income - dollars that get paid over and over to people who've flexed their ingenuity and put it out to the market in different ways.

The thoughts filled Casey with unbridled joy. She reached her next meeting with Elijah brimming with enthusiasm.

"How are you, Casey?"

She beamed, "Fantastic, Elijah. Thank you."

"What's got you so excited?" he asked.

"Until now," she began, "all of this has felt very 'conceptual' to me. I understood it all on an intellectual level. And I believed in the possibilities you'd laid out about Dollar Farming. But it wasn't until I sat down to really think about - and explore the ways in which real people have earned tremendous success by developing Creative Dollar Farms that it struck me: 'this is real. This could be me'."

Elijah smiled.

She continued, "I started by looking up different creators to see if I could find real life examples of successful Creative Dollar Farms. I started with 'self-published' authors and their success stories. I had no idea that Margaret Atwood - the author of my favorite book, *Handmaid's Tale* got her start by self-publishing. I was shocked. But there were so many more. *50 Shades of Grey* was originally self published. So were *The Martian, Eragon, Legally Blonde,* and *The Celestine Prophecy*! Another author, Hugh Howey published a series of books on *Kindle Direct Publishing* that earned him over $150,000 *per month!*

Casey was nearly breathless now. She continued, "And that doesn't even take into account the hundreds of wildly successful non-fiction books I came across. Books about business, meditation, personal finance, fitness, religion, philosophy. You name it!"

Elijah clapped, "Bravo!"

Casey and Elijah sat in a textile print factory. Dozens of massive ink tubs were scattered across a vacuous space that measured hundreds of thousands of square feet. Robotic arms stretched across, plucking fabrics from bins and sorting them down lines to be cut, dyed, and pressed. Casey looked at the spectacle, in awe as people working in tandem with the robots seemed to move with symphonic precision.

"Beyond the world of self-publishing, I dug into a bunch of the other Creative farms we discussed. For example, I learned that some of the most successful musical artists in the world today got their start as independents not signed to a traditional record deal. Many have continued to remain independent. Artists like Frank Ocean and Chance the Rapper. And Billie Eilish and her brother Finneas who you'd mentioned earlier. I found other musical artists who were able to get a song placed on a TV show and then have that success parlay over to build a following on their Spotify accounts. These are truly independent, self-made musicians who have created their own Dollar Farms."

Elijah smiled.

She continued, "I learned about the number of Creators who have built massive followings on YouTube and as a result, significant Dollar Farms. But beyond the mega successful channels like *MrBeast* or *Dude Perfect* who have more than 100 million subscribers, there are hundreds of channels that do incredibly well for everyday creators. There are YouTube channels that are explicitly intended for comedic entertainment while others might be travel oriented. Some are about food & cooking while others are philosophical in nature. Nominally successful YouTube channels can earn thousands of dollars each month. And the really, really successful channels earn *tens of millions a year.* There's no shortage of YouTube millionaires in the world. There's no limit as to what type of video creator you can be or how well you can do."

"I love that you're using the word 'creators'," he said.

"Thanks," Casey replied, "in fact, I learned that a common term for people like those who have YouTube channels and podcasts are 'Content Creators'. It parallels so well with this being the 'Creative' type of farm. Which got me thinking a lot about the last type of 'Creative' farm we'd discussed - education and online classes."

"What are your thoughts?" Elijah asked.

"At first, I really didn't think of that as being in the 'Creative' space. It seems so different from writing, music-making, and video production," she answered. "But then I remembered how we defined the category - it's where the product or service itself is the 'idea' or 'intellectual property' that a customer is paying for. And in that regard, it really is a 'Creative' farm."

"I understand how this can be a bit challenging. Not everything will fit neatly into the somewhat crude analogies we've created with Dollar Farming," he said. "But that fact shouldn't diminish the ultimate objective which is to find ways to create recurring revenue."

"I agree. I looked up courses on Udemy and Skillshare like you'd mentioned. And there really are all sorts of classes that a student can use to increase their knowledge. Some of the classes have hundreds of thousands of reviews which would mean that the Farmer that posted them is earning significant amounts of passive income."

She smiled, then continued, "And I also visited your wife's site. Rebecca is an amazing artist and visiting her site opened my eyes to much more than just her courses."

"What do you mean?" Elijah asked.

"Well, she obviously offers a broad range of lessons and ways for students to access them. Painting techniques for beginners all the way to advanced lessons. A prospective student can buy a class one at a time. But they can buy classes in so many other ways. She creates bundles, subscription packages, and membership tiers," Casey explained. "So the first thing that struck me was how - pardon the pun - 'creative' she is with regards to creating value propositions for her students. There's a way for anyone to buy her courses."

"I'm glad you recognized that," he acknowledged. "It's important to not only think about ways your farm can derive revenue for yourself but also ways that it can be accessible to its customers."

"The other thing that really stood out to me, though, was how her website isn't only geared towards the online courses she offers but how there are so many other Dollar Farms built into it," Casey explained. "And my sense is that in addition to being a 'Creative' farmer, she is also a fantastic 'Commerce' farmer."

Elijah smiled.

"So I was wondering - is that the type of Farm we'll be discussing next?" Casey asked as she looked around at the warehouse where they sat. She watched the workers and machines buzz about, dipping fabrics into dyes and printing logos onto shirts. "And is that why you brought me here?"

He nodded, "You're very intuitive, Casey. Yes, I think it's time to pivot from the 'Creative' category over to 'Commerce'."

**EXERCISE |** Make a list of 'Creative Dollar Farms'. Consider what makes it a Dollar Farm, i.e., how it generates recurring revenue for its farmer. Consider what makes it 'Creative', i.e., why the 'idea' or 'intellectual property' is the item of value that is purchased by the consumer. Then, decide the degree to which this type of Dollar Farm resonates with you. Use the template located at www.TheDollarFarmer.com.

### Chapter 18

# Open 24 / 7 / 365

"In many ways," Elijah said, "I believe the 'Commerce' category will be the most feasible - the most readily accessible - of all the Dollar Farms for new 'Farmers' to start this journey on. Like 'Creative' farms, many of the possible farms in the 'Commerce' category require very little money to get started. So there won't be a large financial barrier to entry for most opportunities. And it can be easily scaled, so profitability is attainable."

"That certainly makes it very intriguing - especially for new Farmers like Jake and me," she smiled.

"Good," he responded. "So in the same way we first defined the '*Creative*' category, let's do that with '*Commerce*' before taking a deeper dive into it. When we say '*Commerce*', what does that mean to you?" he asked.

Casey sat back and pondered, "I've never really thought about it but I suppose that if I had to find a way to simplify it, it just means 'business'."

"'Business' isn't a bad starting point," he responded, "but I want you to be more specific. What do you mean when you say, 'business'?"

She thought about it for a moment. "I suppose I think of it as *'selling stuff'*. I know that sounds dumb, but it's kind of where my head goes. 'Commerce' and 'business' are really just shorthand for *'selling stuff'*."

Elijah chuckled, "You know, I'm not sure I would have originally put it that way, but now that you have, I think it's quite apropos! 'Selling Stuff' is not a bad descriptor for what the 'Commerce' category of Dollar Farming is! In fact," he pulled up his phone, "the 'Oxford Dictionary' defines commerce as 'the activities involved in buying and selling things'."

Casey laughed. "Phew! For a minute, I thought you might kick me out of *Dollar Farming University* for saying something that sounded so ridiculous!"

Elijah shook his head, "I'm glad you were comfortable enough to go out on that limb and say something you were afraid I might not have agreed with. The truth is, we're exploring new terrain. New landscapes. And it's okay to say something that might be at odds with what I'm thinking because we're just spit-balling here and you have plenty to teach me too."

"Thanks Elijah," she said, "So if the crop in a 'Creative' farm is the 'idea' - *the intellectual property* - is it right to say that 'stuff' - *a product* - is the crop in the 'Commerce' farm?"

"For the most part, I think that's absolutely true," Elijah agreed. "You'll find that many of the Dollar Farms in this category are based on selling products large and small of all varieties to customers. That might sound intimidating at first. But in the same way that the barriers of entry for creative types have been shattered, so have the barriers in selling 'stuff'. There are different ways to accomplish this just like there are different types of agriculture on a traditional farm. But you'll find, I think, that ultimately a Dollar Farm that is geared around 'Commerce' is primarily concerned with getting a product and sometimes a service into a customer's hands."

"Are there exceptions to that? Do any 'Commerce' farms not focus on selling stuff?" she asked.

"Of course! With every type of farm, there'll always be exceptions. And there'll always be gray areas - none of this is going to always be black & white, Casey" he remarked. "After all, remember that we're still using imperfect analogies to help us focus and simplify concepts that are complex and abstract. And sometimes, the distinctions between different categories - like 'Creative' and 'Commerce' can be blurred. Some farms might be a little bit of both, for example."

"Understood," Casey said.

"So let's circle back. We started our pivot when you mentioned my wife's website," Elijah recalled. "What were some of the things you noticed there that suggested she may be a 'Commerce' farmer in addition to being a 'Creative' farmer?"

"There were 3 different things on Rebecca's site that jumped out to me as 'Commerce' though I'm not sure if I'm right," she said.

"It's okay if you're wrong," he assured, "Let's see what your instincts tell you."

"First," she said, "I noticed that she had 'stuff' for sale. 'Stuff' like T-shirts, coffee-mugs, and blankets. All with images or catchy phrases that had something to do with her paintings and the classes she teaches."

"Very good," Elijah acknowledged. "She does have an online store where customers can buy 'stuff' related to the painting she does. What else?"

"I also saw that there are links to some of the products she uses and recommends. For example, there are paint brushes and paints that seem to be her preferred products. The visitors on her site can click on the links she provides and buy them at a discount. But I feel like somehow, that must be tied back to revenue for her."

He smiled, "So far, you're 2 for 2. Those are both Dollar Farms in the Commerce category that she's developed. We'll talk about each in more detail but I'm curious as to what you thought of as the third item that is a Dollar Farm on her site."

"Well - I'm not sure how this qualifies," Casey answered, "but I noticed that there were advertisements running on her site. On each page I clicked, ads appeared. I have to imagine that someone pays for those ads just like in a YouTube video or a Podcast. And if she owns the website, she must get paid for those ads."

Elijah sat back with the smile of a proud father. "You aced the test. You just identified 3 of the 'Commerce' Dollar Farms my wife has on her site that generate revenue. That's very impressive. There's another you may not have caught which we'll discuss soon enough but first, let's dive a little deeper into each one of those because they are part of how we'd define the 'Commerce' category."

"Thanks," she replied, "I'm very excited to learn more about these opportunities."

"Let's start with the first farm you mentioned: Rebecca's online store that includes T-shirts, coffee mugs, and other items printed for sale," he said.

"I think that's what we've described in the past as 'Print-On-Demand' or 'POD' for short," Casey added.

Elijah nodded, "That's right. Tell me what you might already know about this type of Dollar Farm."

"I think of it as similar to books in the 'Creative' category in the sense that the item isn't 'made' until someone actually buys it. All kinds of items are available for sale with some sort of artwork or text printed on them and then shipped to a customer," she answered.

"That's a good, basic summary," he said. "You mentioned 'books' which I believe is an interesting parallel. Explain to me how this Dollar Farm mirrors the new world of publishing from a practical point of view."

Casey said, "Once upon a time - and not that long ago - if a person or business wanted to sell merchandise with graphics printed on them, I imagine they'd have to print dozens if not hundreds. That would require a significant investment of the products not to mention the fact that they'd have to be stored somewhere. A warehouse of some sort, I imagine."

"That's exactly right," he answered. "In addition to that, what if a business went through the trouble of printing all of these items only to find that they'd made too many of the wrong size or not enough of a popular design. Constant over and under production would add to the cost of running such a business."

"But with 'Print-On-Demand'," she said, "nothing is printed until a customer decides exactly which graphic design, color, and size of item they want. There is no waste associated with over or under production as you described." Casey smiled before her attention turned to a thought, "One thing I'm not understanding though, is the fact that somewhere, all of those 'blank' items - whether it's T-shirts, mugs, or hats - have to remain stored. So there is an 'inventory' of items somewhere, right?"

"That's true," Elijah answered. "But look around at where we are," he said, motioning to the factory floor where workers, robots, and machines buzzed about.

Different areas and stations performed different jobs. Casey looked closely and saw a worker stretch a blank T-shirt on a pad. After the click of a few buttons on a computer terminal, the T-shirt ran through a machine and came out the other side with a design printed on it. A robotic arm pulled the shirt off the press and dropped it into a crate where it rolled down a line to another station. There, a worker grabbed the shirt, folded it into a packing envelope and dropped it into a bin.

"In some regards, you are correct Casey," Elijah said. "There are still thousands upon thousands of 'blank' items that are made. The difference is that the final product - the one with the graphics - isn't made until a customer makes the purchase. That fundamental difference creates a tremendous amount of operational savings."

"I just realized another way that it creates savings," she said. "Environmentally. Instead of having thousands of items of all types manufactured that might then go unsold, we now have items that are made to order."

"They won't end up in landfills," Elijah said. "I'm so happy you brought that up. This type of Dollar Farm, as is the case with the new world of publishing, is far more sustainable than the traditional processes that were once the only way to market these types of products."

"It will make for a cleaner world," Casey smiled before turning her attention back to the topic at hand, "So how does a person set up this type of business?"

"There are a number of sites that will allow you to create and manage this type of Dollar Farm. Each has their own pros and cons so it would be up to the Dollar Farmer to decide which type is best. But let's discuss a few examples so that you'll get a sense of the different varieties. Let's start with how my wife does it," Elijah said.

He continued, "She created her own website with the help of a web-designer. From there, they embedded an online 'store'. That store exists using an outside service provider. In her case, it's

'Printify' but there are many others such as 'Shopify' and 'Printful' that could also be used. When customers visit her 'store' and find a design on a product they want to buy, they simply add it to their virtual shopping cart, then pay as they check out. Once that happens, an order goes to 'Printify' for fulfillment. 'Printify' has hundreds of partners throughout the world that handle the logistics of printing and shipping the item to the customer. Neither Rebecca nor the customer has any direct involvement with 'Printify' or its fulfillment partners. And Rebecca isn't involved in the production process at all aside from the designs she created."

"And how do those designs end up on the shirts or coffee mugs? I see samples of them on her website," Casey asked.

"Those are digital mock-ups. When someone opens this kind of store, they upload their design, then it is virtually superimposed onto a blank version of the item you're selling. It isn't actually printed on the sample you see even though it appears to be," Elijah explained.

"That's amazing," she said. "And the designs themselves - how are they made? I realize that your wife is an artist so for her it might be easier. But can people who aren't artists also create designs and graphics that would look good on the merchandise?"

"Absolutely!" he answered. "In fact, there are all sorts of graphic design programs and sites that are tailored specifically to people who aren't artists so that they can make a vision come to life. 'Canva' is a very popular one that comes to mind. Anyone - even a person who has never designed any graphics - can go onto a site like Canva and create fantastic designs. Of course, you could also pay a graphic designer the one-time fee of making a design for you."

"Wow," she said, "I'm going to check that out." Casey sat back and watched the workings of the T-shirt factory. It looked like a well choreographed ballet with each of the workers and machines moving with purpose and precision. And it brought her a sense of satisfaction in knowing that every one of the items that was rolling down the conveyor was made specifically for a single customer who'd made the purchase.

"You'd mentioned that there were other ways to have a 'Print-On-Demand' business - one that's different from your wife's," Casey remembered.

"My wife's business runs through her website. It works for her because she's been able to set up a business that brings traffic to her site. But not everyone will have or want that type of business," Elijah explained. "Some Farmers don't already have a 'following' and no desire or willingness to develop one. And some may have a following but want to create a business separate and apart from it. That doesn't mean they can't start this type of POD Dollar Farm for themselves."

"How would that work?" Casey asked.

"There are a number of platforms that provide the ability to upload your own designs and even your own 'store' within their platform. So if a customer logs onto the site looking for example, for a poster or article of clothing with a catchy phrase about something in particular, they can do a search and your item would appear," Elijah explained. "At that point, they select your item and purchase it from the site."

"And then it gets printed and shipped - just like the ones from your wife's website?" she asked.

"That's exactly right," he said. "It's all coordinated - all you need to worry about is coming up with catchy slogans, phrases, and designs that will get people's attention."

"What are some of the sites that allow for something like that?"

Elijah answered, "There are several. 'Red Bubble', 'Teespring', and even 'Etsy' are a few that come to mind."

"I always assumed that 'Etsy' was a site for artisans to sell their art, crafts, and jewelry," she said.

"It is that, but a person can also set up a 'Print-on-Demand' store just like the ones we've been describing and run it through 'Etsy'. The advantage that a site like 'Etsy' has is that it gets a lot of traffic on its own. So there is a good opportunity to have your items found as people search," he explained.

"I can really see the appeal of starting a 'POD' Dollar Farm. There are virtually no costs to getting it started and you are only limited by your creativity," Casey said.

"Absolutely," he agreed. "It is a tremendously accessible opportunity and it runs 24 hours a day, 7 days a week."

"And there's nothing to stop a person from adding new items and designs to their stores," she added.

"That's a great point, Casey," Elijah said. "I often recommend a person set up their store with maybe a half dozen designs or so. Something clever that might appeal to a specific niche. For example, pet-lovers - or even more specifically, dog or cat lovers. Other farmers write catchy phrases about things people enjoy like coffee, wine, or a favorite hobby. In either case, the farmer should find a niche that is fun and appealing to them and set up several designs. Then, continually add new designs. Over time, you'll come to learn what is working and what types of designs or slogans people respond to and buy."

"And each time they do," Casey started, "you get paid."

"That's why we call it 'Dollar Farming'," Elijah smiled. "But the nice takeaway is that trying the different styles and designs didn't 'cost' the farmer lots of wasted inventory."

"I just have to pinch myself and recognize that this kind of business truly can be started by anyone at any time with virtually no financial investment to create a stream of passive, recurring income," Casey exclaimed. "A 65 year-old can start a Print-On-Demand business to generate recurring revenue for themselves."

He nodded, "Absolutely. Like we'd said at the outset, age is not a limitation. For an older person, Dollar Farming is a fantastic way to bridge shortfalls they might have with Social Security and their retirement investments."

"That's true," Casey acknowledged. "What about the other opportunity I saw on your wife's site? The links she had to some of her favorite products?" Casey asked.

Elijah answered, "That is what we call 'Affiliate Marketing' or 'Affiliate Links'. In a nutshell, the Dollar Farmer has a direct, custom web link to a specific company's product. When a person visiting that site - for example, my wife Rebecca's site - clicks the link she's posted and buys the product, Rebecca earns a small commission."

"That's interesting - so she doesn't have to buy the products herself or carry any inventory," she said. "Does this type of farm only work for people who already have the kind of following or audience that Rebecca has?"

"It might be a bit easier, at least initially, for someone who has a following to develop an 'Affiliate Link' business," Elijah said. "But truly, anyone can set up and establish a successful farm of this type. For example," he continued, "a person could set up a YouTube channel geared specifically towards 'reviewing' different types of products. Then, viewers of the reviews could purchase those products by clicking links in the descriptions. I've seen other people make social media accounts that are geared towards a very specific type of audience. For example, funny cat videos. Then, every dozen posts or so, they'll post a product directed to that market. Like a cat toy or brush."

"So it seems that if you find a certain niche that you can cultivate to build an audience over time, it would help," Casey considered.

"I think that is absolutely true. And it's probably true for just about any Dollar Farm we discuss," he said. "Most businesses in general are more successful when they know who their target customer is rather than trying to be all things to all people."

"I bet that's where 'Passion' in the MAP process really helps," she surmised. "Someone who really loves boating or surfing or cats should maybe seek their niche in one of those loves rather than something they have no connection to."

"Like my wife and her art," Elijah agreed.

"And how does somebody go about getting those links you were talking about?"

"There are several ways," he answered. "In some cases, you can approach the company directly. But what is much more common is to use existing online stores. For example, Amazon has an affiliate program. So does Walmart."

"I never realized that by clicking the links on a web page that takes me to Amazon, that it would generate a commission for someone," she said.

"It sure does," he replied. "The other way that is very effective for this type of business is to align with a platform that is geared specifically for Affiliate marketing. These are sites like 'Clickbank' and 'ShareASale' that have affiliated vendors and merchants who work directly with them and the Dollar Farmers. From there a pro-spective farmer can create the link that will connect back to their own website as Rebecca has done and then drive sales of those products."

"But this sounds a little like being a commissioned salesper-son," she observed.

"If you think of it as a commission you get for each sale of a product, it would seem that way," he acknowledged. "But what makes it very different is that the Dollar Farmer isn't physically having to direct each sale. Rather, they create a marketing mechanism which in turn generates sales over and over and over again."

"So it's the marketing mechanism you mentioned which is in some ways the Dollar Farm - or at least the fertile soil from which the crop is harvested," Casey replied.

"Very keen observation," Elijah said. "And there are many different ways to go about creating that marketing mechanism. It can be a website, a YouTube Channel, a podcast, a blog, Social Media pages. The idea is to find a way to feature the benefits of a product that people will like and would want to click through and buy."

Casey said, "That makes perfect sense. So for Rebecca, her website and her expertise as an artist is the marketing mechanism. People who take her courses and watch her videos come to trust her recommendations. As a result, they are willing to buy the products she's 'endorsed'. Almost like a celebrity spokesperson."

"Yes, the credibility that a person gains as an 'expert' in their field allows them to put that credibility to work in recommending products and services - particularly if it's in a field associated with their area of expertise," Elijah said. "But it is of utmost importance that a person guard their reputation by only making recommendations for products that they actually believe in themselves."

"I completely understand that," she agreed. "A person can destroy their reputation - and any future credibility by recommending substandard products. Not only does that strike me as unethical - it will ruin their ability to keep making sales. Rebecca seems to have a sterling reputation which is why I'm sure she's able to get so many visits to her website. And how she's able to also utilize it for advertising - the 3rd 'Commerce' farm I saw there."

"Yes - any website can be monetized, that is, have ads running which can generate revenue. Of course, the more traffic a website has, the higher revenue it can command for advertising - especially for ads that pay for 'click-through'."

"What's that?" she asked.

"Click-through ads are those that, similar to 'Affiliate links', pay the website owner any time someone 'clicks' on their ad. The only difference is that a sale of the product isn't required in this case for the website owner to earn a bit of revenue," he said. "This is one of those exceptions we mentioned - where even though it's a 'Commerce' farm, it isn't geared around 'selling stuff', per se. The 'stuff' in this farm are the advertisements."

"So Rebecca uses her website as a hub to run multiple Dollar Farms: her classes which can be paid for individually or in bulk, a Print-On-Demand business, Affiliate links for products she recommends, and the website itself for advertising revenue," Casey observed. "You'd mentioned there was another Dollar Farm that I might have overlooked. What was it?"

"I'm glad you'd remembered that," Elijah smiled. "Nestled somewhere in between her 'Print-On-Demand' products that include T-shirts and coffee mugs and the affiliate links for the paints she recommends are another set of products she sells: paint brushes."

"That's funny - I'd noticed the paint brushes," Casey said. "I just assumed they were a brand she was recommending via an affiliate link."

"Nope," Elijah smiled, "They are actually brushes that she herself sells."

"What do you mean?" she asked. "She has a garage-full of paint brushes?"

"Heavens no!" he laughed. "It's a type of Dollar Farm called 'Dropshipping'."

"Dropshipping? What's that?" she asked.

He answered, "Dropshipping has several similarities with Print-On-Demand. Like sister and brother farms. They both allow the farmer to have a product sold and shipped directly to a customer. The farmer never has to carry inventory of the product and usually won't have to pay for it until a customer makes the sale. So in this regard, there is virtually no up-front investment or expense to the farmer."

"Let me see if I understand so far: a customer finds a product they want to buy on the farmer's website store or social media page, buys it, has it delivered straight to them and the farmer gets paid," Casey surmised.

"That's right," he said.

"So how is that different from Print-On-Demand?"

"The primary differences are, in my view, two-fold: firstly, with Print-On-Demand, the farmer is creating the custom graphic that will be added to the product. With Dropshipping on the other hand, the product is already in its complete form. No design work needs to be added to it," he said. Elijah continued, "The second difference is that Print-On-Demand has a much narrower range of products to choose from. After all, there are only so many types of items that one would add custom graphics to. But with Dropshipping, virtually anything you can think of can be an item that can be sold this way. From office supplies to yoga mats to shower curtains."

Casey asked, "So how does a farmer earn revenue in Dropshipping?"

"The way most conventional stores make money is by purchasing products from a manufacturer or distributor at 'bulk' prices - what we'd call 'wholesale'. Then, they add a 'markup' to the price which is now sold as 'retail'. Dropshipping works the same way. As a general matter, a Dropshipper pays 'wholesale' prices for a product from a manufacturer or distributor, then sells them at 'retailer' prices. Usually, the mark-up can be anywhere from 3 to 10 times what they paid for them," he answered. "The Dollar Farmer gets paid the difference between the wholesale price they paid and the retail price they sell it for."

"Wow - I would have never thought of that!" she remarked. "The brush sets on Rebecca's site that sell for $20 only cost her $6?"

"Maybe even less than that. And that difference is the profit she keeps," Elijah said.

"So how does a person get started with a dropshipping business?" Casey asked.

"Like Print-On-Demand, there are several different ways to go about it," Elijah explained. "The way Rebecca did it is probably among the most common. She created a 'Shopify' store on her website then, used their app, 'Oberlo' which allows her to search for the types of products she wants to sell, find the suppliers for those products, then allows her to add them seamlessly to her online store. The suppliers usually come via 'AliExpress' which is a global network of manufacturers and suppliers."

"It really is remarkable," Casey said. "Obviously, it makes sense for her to sell products that her art students would want. But for someone like me, maybe I would get into the yoga niche since it's something I enjoy. And someone like Jake could create a store that would cater to gearheads like he is."

"Absolutely," Elijah agreed. "There is virtually no limit. But there are a couple of very important considerations when it comes to Dropshipping. The first is that to do it in the way I described, fulfillment times are usually longer than with Print-On-Demand since the products are often coming from overseas factories. So whereas a POD customer might receive their custom graphic T-shirt in a week or so, a Dropship product might take as long as a month to arrive. That's why you as the business owner need to be able to manage client expectations."

"Especially in a world where people are accustomed to 2-Day deliveries from places like Amazon," she said.

"Which leads to another way to run a Dropshipping business," he said. "Other Dropshippers are comfortable and prefer the idea of buying inventory up front from suppliers rather than waiting for the 'buy as you sell' model I described just now. In this scenario, a dropship farmer identifies the product and supplier they want to use, then place a large, wholesale order and have the products shipped to an 'Amazon Fulfillment Center'. There, the farmer will pay a 'storage and handling fee' to Amazon but once that's done, Amazon can place the prized 'Prime' badge on the product. Then, when a customer buys it, Amazon handles the shipping directly to the customer using its 2 day 'Prime' model which also means returns will be handled by them. It's what's referred to as 'Fulfillment by Amazon'."

"So let me see if I understand this correctly - under the first method you described, I as the Dollar Farmer wouldn't have to 'pay' for an item until it is sold so there is virtually no start-up cost. And there are no inventory concerns. That's an advantage. However, it could take weeks for my customer to get their product," Casey summarized. "On the other hand, if I'm willing to take the chance and make the financial investment, I can purchase the products in bulk and have them shipped to an Amazon warehouse, pay a fee, but let Amazon take care of the shipping."

"That's exactly right," he said. "My general suggestion for someone starting out - especially if they don't have a budget or an established niche yet - is to go with option one at first, get their feet wet, and find out what sells best and most. Then, if they have enough success and money, they can 'graduate' to the FBA platform if they choose to."

"That makes a lot of sense," Casey agreed.

"I'm glad you visited Rebecca's website," Elijah said. "It really helped create a great way to explore the 'Commerce' category."

"Are there any other types of farms that might fall into the 'Commerce' category that we didn't talk about?" she asked.

"There are, and like the 'Creative' category, there'll be new ones invented with every passing year," he said. "But I think the ones we explored - 'Dropshipping', 'Print-On-Demand', 'Affiliate Link Marketing', and 'Ad-based revenue' are the fundamental ones to understand in this category. As you become more of an explorer, you might identify others you like. But you now have a foundation."

She smiled, "So does that mean we're ready to get to the last category, 'Capital'?"

"It sure does," he nodded.

EXERCISE | Make a list of 'Commerce Dollar Farms'. Consider what makes it a Dollar Farm, i.e., how it generates recurring revenue for its farmer. Consider what makes it 'Commerce', i.e., what is the item of value that is purchased by the consumer on a recurring basis. Then, decide the degree to which this type of Dollar Farm resonates with you. Use the template located at www.TheDollarFarmer.com.

## Chapter 19

# The Cash Machine

The next week, Elijah agreed to meet Casey at her yoga gym. After an invigorating workout, they went to a smoothie bar for their next conversation. Normally, a yoga session calmed Casey's mind but she'd spent the last few days with her head spinning. She'd observed the world around her and was awestruck at how 'new' everything suddenly seemed. She started to see opportunities at every corner.

She thought to herself, "*I could write a 'How-To' book on Marketing. Or maybe start a YouTube channel about 'Yoga for Beginners'. And we could use that to sell yoga stuff like mats and T-Shirts with slogans geared towards practitioners and enthusiasts. Maybe Jake and I can start a Video Log - a VLOG about travel and put that on YouTube. Of course aside from his mechanical stuff, Jake loves cooking - so he could have his own YouTube channel about that? Or a cookbook....so many possibilities... it's overwhelming...*"

After taking a sip of her matcha tea smoothie, she peered up. "Elijah?"

He noticed the anxiousness welling on her face. "What's up, Casey?"

"I have so many thoughts - so many possibilities dancing in my head that I'm starting to feel overwhelmed. I'm excited about Dollar Farming but am also getting so confused," she expressed.

"I understand," he said. "We've pulled back the curtains on a whole new world - one you had never even considered and while it's exciting, it can also feel like a bit too much. Like going to a restaurant and being handed a 100 page menu."

She chuckled. "Yeah, there's almost too much to choose from. And we haven't even spoken about the 'Capital' category yet."

"I get it. But it's also why we discussed the MAP process before. So that you could parse through the almost endless list of possibilities and eventually curate the types of Dollar Farms that would be right for you. We want to narrow a 100 page menu down to 2 or 3 entree items that appeal to you and Jake," he explained.

"That makes sense," Casey exhaled. "And I keep thinking about how your wife Rebecca has multiple Dollar Farms that she runs. Do we have to start with so many? Or could we start with just one?"

"Of course! You can start with a single Dollar Farm and add on as you go - *if you choose to*. Some farmers are content with a single, successful farm though I am a big advocate of having multiple farms - certainly more than one or two if possible."

"Why is that?" she asked.

"*Income diversity* will be an area that we want to explore. Knowing that if one or two of your income farms struggle for whatever reason - be it a change in market environment or a shift in the economy - other revenue streams will still provide for your needs and lifestyle," he said.

"That there'll always be enough '*Flow*'," Casey added.

"Exactly. For example, I started with a single Dollar Farm and now, I have over a dozen different Dollar Farms that I currently tend to."

"Wow! I can't imagine juggling that many businesses. How is that even possible?!" she exclaimed.

"I'm sure the thought of it is overwhelming for you right now. But *how* to build and sustain multiple dollar farms will be a topic we explore in more detail when we get to the 5th 'F' in the program," Elijah said. "For now, let's focus on our task-at-hand: discussing the next category on our list: 'Capital'."

"Sounds good, Elijah. Sorry to have gotten off track," she said.

"No need to apologize at all - this is an open discussion and I'm happy you're allowing yourself the freedom to think broadly and ask questions," he consoled.

Casey smiled.

"So tel v" he said.

"I suppose that in the same way I thought of *'Commerce'* as 'selling stuff', I think of *'Capital'* quite simply as 'money'," she surmised.

Elijah answered, "That's a pretty good starting point. And in general, I'd agree that it's what you'd need to start a 'Capital' Farm. Money is the 'seed', so-to-speak."

"But there's more to it," she suspected.

"Correct," he said.

Casey thought, "Hmm. I suppose it isn't the 'money' itself but rather what you do with that money. What you buy with it."

"Bingo. In a *'Capital'* Farm, money is used or rather, *invested to purchase and own an income-generating asset*," Elijah explained.

She said, "So at the risk of oversimplifying, a *'Creative'* farm is in the business of *selling ideas*, a *'Commerce'* farm is in the business of *selling stuff*, and a *'Capital'* farm is in the business of *owning stuff*."

"Kudos!" he exclaimed, "That's a very insightful way to look at each of them."

"And how in some ways, the 'Commerce' category really is a sort of hybrid of the other two," Casey added.

"Excellent point," Elijah said.

She re-drew the venn diagram:

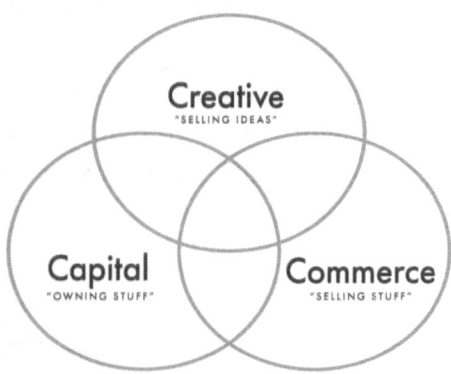

"Fantastic, Casey," Elijah remarked, "So now that we know what it is on a general level, let's talk about some specific different types of assets that generate income as well as the barriers to entry of this type of farm."

"I imagine that the biggest barrier to entry is the money itself. A person needs the seed money just to get started," she said.

"That's absolutely true," he agreed. "The biggest challenge that most farmers will encounter in the 'Capital' type - at least initially - is the money they'd need to get started. And some farms in this category can require a fairly sizable investment. However," he continued, "in many cases, there are work-arounds and in other cases, the investment is not overwhelming. I think you'll find there are still opportunities here for would-be farmers who don't have a tremendous amount of excess cash on hand."

"That's encouraging," she said.

"There are all sorts of farms available in this category. And in most ways, it represents the most 'traditional' types of Dollar Farming," Elijah began.

"That's interesting," Casey opined. "I wonder why that is."

"If you think about it, there's a fundamental reason for that," he said. "When you look back at the 'Creative' and 'Commerce' categories, what were some of the things we discussed that made them viable now in ways they weren't possible even a generation ago?"

"As I think back on them, I realize we spoke a lot about how many of the farms that fall into those categories have been facilitated or made possible by advances in technology," she said. "For example, 'Print-On-Demand' - whether we're talking about a T-Shirt or a book. The way Video Creators can post on YouTube and marketers can use 'Affiliate Links' to sell products. All of these businesses are made possible by the internet, automation, and a globally connected world."

"That's exactly right," Elijah agreed. "Many of these farms were simply not existent - or certainly not as available just a decade or two ago." He sipped from his smoothie before continuing, "On the other hand, many of the farms we'll look at in the 'Capital' category have been around for decades and in some cases, hundreds or even thousands of years."

"Thousands of years? Does that mean they run the risk of becoming outdated?" she asked.

"Good question. My sense is that any industry *can* become obsolete in the blink of an eye when something revolutionary comes along to displace it. The way cars made the horse and buggy obsolete. And CDs displaced the cassette and record industries before themselves being replaced by streaming," he explained. "But in general, these farms don't seem to be at risk any more than any other even though they in many ways pre-date the more modern ones we've been discussing."

Elijah paused for a moment before continuing, "And what's more important than focusing on any one of these specific farms is to remember that we're *retraining our minds* on how we view our relationship to how we generate income. Some of these farms will go - they'll be replaced. And new ones will emerge. But if you always remember the goal..."

"...to not trade time for dollars..." she interjected.

"...then you'll do fine, regardless of how businesses, economies, and industries change," he finished.

They took a moment to smile in appreciation of the lessons they'd learned so far before Elijah continued, "So tell me, Casey - what are some of the different types of 'assets' that might produce recurring revenue?"

Casey replied, "I think in that first conversation we had, we discussed a few. I specifically remember ATMs and apartment listings. I think these would all qualify for the 'Capital' category, right?"

Elijah nodded, "I agree. They are very different from each other in many ways. Yet, they ultimately require the farmer to invest capital in an asset - the ATM machine or the apartment - to have it then generate regularly recurring income."

"The old adage," she said, "it takes money to make money."

"In this case, that adage holds some truth," he said. "It's also why a different kind of evaluation needs to be made by the farmer prior to plunging into the 'Capital' category. The farmer needs to consider what their 'return on investment' will be, or 'ROI' as it's known in business lingo."

"Return on Investment. What does that mean?" she asked.

"Oftentimes, 'Capital' farms will lack liquidity. That's a fancy way of saying that once you've bought the capital asset, you can't get your money back out of it easily. So when a 'farmer' makes the investment to purchase the asset - the 'stuff they'll own' - they need to consider how much money that investment will make and how long it would take to get their investment back. That's what ROI means in basic terms."

"I gotcha," she understood, "if I buy an ATM machine for say $3000, ROI would tell me how long it would take for me to make that money back and start earning a profit."

"That's right," he answered, "and another consideration with these types of farms is that they'll often have 'carrying costs'."

"Do you mean an ongoing cost associated with owning the 'thing'?" Casey asked.

"Correct. So a farmer must evaluate how the revenue stream will pay for the initial investment and whether the amount it generates regularly will be offset by the costs associated in owning and running it," Elijah finished.

"I see how this is a bit different from the farms in the 'Creative' and 'Commerce' categories. Those don't seem to have much of an initial investment or ongoing carrying costs," she said.

"As a general matter, that's true. There are always exceptions but for the most part, starting and maintaining 'Creative' and 'Commerce' farms will require a farmer make less of an initial outlay and less in the way of ongoing spending," he said. "You mentioned a few examples of farms that fall into the 'Capital' category," Elijah continued. "Can you think of any others?"

"Hmm," she considered the question as she sipped from her smoothie, "I hate to say that nothing really comes to mind, Elijah."

"What did you just do?" he asked.

"What do you mean?" Casey replied.

"While you were pondering the question," he said, "*you did something.*"

She thought about it a moment before answering, "I took a sip of my smoothie. Is that what you mean?"

Elijah smiled. "That's exactly right."

She seemed perplexed, "My smoothie is a Dollar Farm?"

He laughed. "Not the smoothie itself," he replied. "But where are we now? This place where we got our smoothies?"

"Uh...a smoothie shop," she answered, still a bit hesitant and not quite sure of how this related to Dollar Farming.

"I recognize this feels a bit less clear-cut," Elijah said. "But think about it, there's a 'person' who owns this smoothie store. And if they've set things up correctly..."

"...then it will generate recurring revenue for them," she understood. "Wow - it's hard for me to think of a place like this as a Dollar Farm. But I think I understand what you mean."

"Not just a place like this. I agreed to visit your yoga gym earlier partially because I wanted to enjoy the experience of the workout but also because it is another example of this type of business. This type of Dollar Farm," he said.

"I would have never thought of that," Casey realized.

"We'll take a deeper dive in just a moment," he said. "But first, let's take a big picture look at these examples to see if we can identify them as different types of 'Capital' farms."

"Okay. So we've got a smoothie shop, an ATM machine, and a rental apartment," she reported. "I agree, they all require a financial investment to own but they are all very different."

Elijah nodded, "Indeed they are. And I think they're great examples of 3 of the different types of 'Capital' farms we'll discuss."

"So there are 3 types in this 'Capital' category?" Casey asked.

"There are actually 4 from my perspective," he answered, "but we won't get to the last one just yet."

She smiled, "Now you've got me intrigued."

"Good! So let's look at these 3 first. How would you describe each of them categorically?"

Casey thought about it before answering, "An ATM is a machine that generates income for its owner. An apartment is a piece of real-estate. And a smoothie shop is a business. So, 'machine', 'real-estate', and 'business'."

Elijah clapped, "Bravo! You nailed it!"

"Really?" she blushed.

"Absolutely! Those are the first 3, fundamental types of farms in the 'Capital' category: 'Machines', 'Real Estate', and 'Business'," he said. "Let's look into each one of those a bit more closely."

"Sounds good," she said. "So to start, I can be a Dollar Farmer by buying 'machines'?"

"Correct. Machines that provide a product or service which customers will pay for over and over. Let's define the 'Machine' type," he said. "What do you think it entails?"

"When I think of an ATM, I think of a machine that charges a fee to a customer who is withdrawing money," she answered.

"That's very good," he said. "Not all machines will be this explicit in the way they generate revenue. But the basic premise is sound: a customer is paying for something that the machine dispenses or provides. An ATM is a perfect example," he continued, "In fact - it has 'machine' in its name. Automated Teller Machine - ATM."

They laughed. "The job of the Dollar Farmer in this example is to buy the ATM and find a strategic place where would-be customers come to withdraw money. The Dollar Farmer's only ongoing responsibilities are to make sure it is 'loaded' with inventory - in this case cash for withdrawals - and that it is in good working order."

After smiling, Elijah leaned in and whispered, "And that is the secret sauce for just about every 'machine' oriented Dollar Farm. Buy it, place it, keep it loaded, and working."

She laughed, "That seems eerily simple."

"I am, of course, oversimplifying it," he said. "But not by much. 'Machine' farms are built around the idea that there are 'things' or 'services' people need or want and are willing to pay for the convenience they provide. Can you think of any other 'machines' you could buy that serve a similar function?"

"We'd talked about a 'car wash'," she answered. "I think it would fall into that category."

"I agree. It's different in the sense that the customer doesn't pay an explicit 'fee' to use it. But obviously, as long as the car wash owner charges a fee above the operational expenses of the wash, they keep the difference. This is their profit," he said. "Any others?"

"The most obvious example that comes to mind are vending machines. And once again, the answer is in its name," she smiled.

"Good," he acknowledged. "I think you get the gist of the 'machine' type of farm. Anywhere anyone goes to deposit money or pay a fee for a dispensed product or service, you're looking at a 'machine' farm."

"So slot machines fall into this category too," she laughed.

"That's exactly right...In many regards, I look at casinos as big money Dollar Farms. Of course the slot machines. But the poker and black jack tables are also Dollar Farms. In a way, they are all little machine farms too," he said.

"But the blackjack and poker tables have dealers working them. They're not machines," she said.

He smiled, "You're right and I don't intend to dehumanize the dealers. I was just emphasizing the point that like most Machine farms, a customer walks in, deposits their money for a product or service - in the case of a casino, the cost of gambling entertainment, and the owner keeps the profits."

"But wouldn't that example be true of any business? Not just a casino?"

"Hold your thought, Casey," Elijah nodded, "we'll actually circle back to exactly that when we discuss the fifth 'F'. For now, we'll stay on topic. I think you get the gist of a 'Machine' farm in the 'Capital' category."

"I think so," she answered. "Invest in a machine that dispenses a product or service in exchange for money that the customer is willing to deposit into it. Since it works 'automatically', the owner gets paid over and over without having to tend to each transaction. Perfect example of a Dollar Farm."

"That it is," he said. "So now that we've covered that, let's look at the next example: where does the machine in one of those Dollar Farms sit?"

"I guess in a property," she said.

"Exactly," he countered. "Which leads to our next 'Capital' farm: 'Real Estate'. This may seem like a fairly self-explanatory category but it can be tricky and there's a lot of potential nuance. We'll spend quite a bit of time going through this type. Tell me what you'd think of when we consider a 'Real Estate' Dollar Farm?"

"I think the most obvious answer is what we've discussed: someone buys a piece of property - maybe a house or apartment, then rents it out to someone else. The owner - the Dollar Farmer - keeps the profit above and beyond the ongoing expense of owning the property," Casey answered.

"In a nutshell, you've said it just right," he said. "A property rental is the most basic example of a real estate farm. A landlord with a properly situated rental can have a steady stream of income for life."

"Landlords and tenants," she remarked. "Earlier, you'd said that some of these 'Capital' farms have been around for thousands of years. This is one of them, isn't it?"

He nodded, "Landowners have generated recurring revenue for millenia. And like I said earlier, that is unlikely to change anytime soon."

"And realistically, there's nothing to stop a person from owning 'multiple' properties. You could have more than one, right?" she observed.

"Of course - we'll get to that in a moment. But before doing so, let's look at how a 'real estate' farm gets set up and becomes operational. The first step is in deciding what type of rental you'd want to own. Will it be a long-term or short-term rental?"

"Long-term or short-term?" she asked. "I'm not sure I understand."

"I suppose when you think of a rental property, you imagine a person who will come and live in the place for a year or two. Maybe longer," Elijah said.

"That's right," Casey agreed. "I'd buy a place, then find a nice person or family to rent it out to. They'd live there a long time, I'd hope."

"And that's a perfect example of a 'long-term' rental. Someone who will spend more than just a few days or weeks in the property," he said. "But what if a person is going on vacation and visiting a city for a few nights? What choices do they have now aside from booking a hotel?"

"Of course!" she laughed. "They can get an 'AirBnB' or a 'VRBO'!"

"Correct," he said. "Those are examples of 'short-term' rentals.

A 'Real Estate' farmer can buy a property with the intention specifically geared towards that type of renter."

"Which is better?" Casey asked.

"There is no 'better' or 'worse'," he answered. "There are just different considerations. Each has its own pros and cons. Its own risks and rewards. And by the way, that's true of every type of Dollar Farm. Which is why each Dollar Farmer might decide for themselves *which is a better farm for them* - but not that it's necessarily a better farm in general."

"I understand - just like someone might prefer to start a YouTube channel where someone else will sell T-Shirts online. And yet another person will rent a house out on AirBnB," she acknowledged.

"And yet even still another person will do all three," Elijah said.

"Gotcha. So what are some of the pros and cons of short-term versus long-term rentals?" she asked.

"There are a few considerations. Usually, a person that rents a property out short-term will make more on a per night basis than the person renting long-term," he answered. "But they'll have to accept the probability of more vacancies. More nights where the unit is not rented."

"So if I want the security of knowing that I won't have to worry about constant turnover and possibly lots of vacant nights where the unit is not generating money, then a long-term property might be more up my alley," Casey said.

"That's right," he said, "but on the flip side, if you are able to manage and market your short-term rental well, you have an opportunity to make a good bit more money with it. And if you ever want to access to the property for your own use, a short-term strategy might be better."

"How so?" she asked.

"For example," Elijah said, "Rebecca and I own an apartment

in Barcelona. We rent it out on AirBnB and because we bought in a desirable area and offer it at a reasonable price, it's rented out most nights. But if she and I ever want a little European getaway, we block out those dates and know we have a place to stay in one of the world's most magnificent cities."

"That's so cool! What a dream. I wish Jake and I could do that!" she said.

"*You can*," Elijah said. "You just have to start thinking like a Dollar Farmer. The dream is not so far away."

"You're right - it's not," Casey smiled. "Thank you, Elijah. So how does one go about buying a rental property? And turning it into a Dollar Farm?"

"For starters, you'd need to gather the funds for a down payment. Usually, for an investment property, it's at least 15% of the property value. Sometimes more. Then, you'd need to qualify for a mortgage - a loan - for the amount that needs to be financed."

"Just like buying a house," she said. "Jake and I recently bought our first home and that's what we did."

"Perfect," he said. "On a basic level, that's what you'd do for a rental property. The only big differences are that normally, the interest rate you'd pay for the loan on an investment property would be higher than for your own home because the bank lending you the money is assuming larger risks for a property that the owner won't be living in full-time."

Elijah took a sip of his smoothie, then continued, "So you, as the owner, have to take that into account when renting the property out. You'll have larger 'overhead' so you have to make sure the rent you charge will cover it. And in your homework, you'd have to make sure before you make the investment, that whatever you'll charge is reasonable relative to the rental market."

"That's a great point," she said. "It'd be a disaster buying a property, then after mortgage and insurance payments, having to charge someone more than what other properties in the area are going for. That would be a horrible mistake."

"Exactly," he said. "It's all part of the homework a real estate farmer needs to do before making the investment. It's what you'd do in the 'Arrange' part of the process."

"It seems like it'd be hard to become a real estate farmer with the large, up-front investment it would require," Casey said. "Properties often cost hundreds of thousands of dollars. A person would need tens of thousands of dollars just for the down payment."

"Traditionally, that's true," he acknowledged. "And that's still going to be the best way for most real estate farmers to get in the game to do it in the most profitable and effective way possible. But let me offer you a few alternatives - *ways to think creatively* as a Dollar Farmer who'd like to get started in real estate."

"I'm all ears," she said.

"The most basic way for a new Dollar Farmer to get their feet wet in real estate is to do something called 'House Hacking'," he said.

"House Hacking? What's that?"

"Instead of buying a separate property to rent out," Elijah explained, "a house hacker rents out part of the property they reside in. For example, if you own a three bedroom house, you'd rent one or two of the other bedrooms to tenants. Or another possibility is buying a multi-unit building, living in one, and renting the others out."

"I would have never thought of that!" Casey exclaimed. "So you are essentially getting someone else to pay your mortgage for you."

"And because you are an owner-occupant of the property, the mortgage qualifies for a lower interest rate," Elijah added. "Furthermore, using a conventional or FHA loan instead of a loan to secure an investment property, the borrower can sometimes get away with putting as little as 3% down. So a much lower initial investment and lower carrying costs."

"That's ingenious!"

"House hacking is a great way for a person to become a real estate Dollar Farmer," he said. "But let me give you another example where a person with relatively little money can get 'in the game', so-to-speak."

Casey smiled, "This is getting interesting. I can see myself as a real estate farmer!"

"Good," he said. "There are sites and tools a person can use to find out where AirBnB and VRBOs are renting most successfully. Sites like 'AirDNA' and 'Mashvisor' that allow a prospective farmer to decide what city or locale they might want to invest in," he said. "Then, after setting up a Limited Liability Corporation - an LLC - you'd find a nice unit in a condominium or apartment building and sign a corporate lease."

"An LLC? A corporate lease?" she asked. "This got intense quickly."

He laughed, "Stay with me, Casey. It's not as difficult as it might sound. And remember: you're a business owner now - you have to think like one. Business owners protect themselves by running their businesses as such. And to do so, you'll set yourself up by owning a business. For most people starting out, the cheapest and easiest way is to set up an LLC. It only costs a few hundred dollars but will be among the best investments in yourself and your farming business you'll ever make. And by the way, setting up an LLC would be something you do for *any* type of farm - not just the one I'm about to share."

"Ok - I'll go with it for now. I've set up an LLC like you said. Now what?"

"Good," he said, "In this scenario, you'll set up the LLC and because you're operating as a 'business' - not as an individual known as 'Casey', you can get a corporate lease in apartment buildings that allow it. You pay the first month's rent and another month for the security deposit. Let's pretend those are $2000 each."

"Okay - I'm following. I'm out of pocket $4000 plus the cost of setting up an LLC," Casey said. "Then what?"

"Then you'd spend another two or three thousand to furnish it. You're out of pocket less than $10,000," Elijah said. "And your carrying costs are only $2000 a month."

"Okay, Elijah. You've got my attention," she said. "Now what?"

He smiled, "Now, you rent it on a short-term basis - AirBNB for example - for $4000 a month to high quality tenants who might need it for just a few weeks at a time. Like travel nurses and insurance claimants. If you did that, how does the math work out?" he asked.

"I'd be netting $2000 a month in profit," she calculated.

"Correct," Elijah acknowledged. "Now here's a perfect case where we explore our prior conversation about 'Return on Investment."

"ROI," she added. "Okay. Let's figure out how quickly this could be profitable. Between the first month's rent, security deposit, and furnishing, it cost me about $7000. Then $2000 each month in rent thereafter. If I rent it for $4000 each month so I'm profiting $2000 each of those months, how quickly would I break even? How soon would I start making money on my investment?"

"Good. You're starting to think like a business person. Like a true Dollar Farmer," he said. "Let's do what I call 'cocktail napkin math'."

He grabbed a paper napkin from the smoothie bar counter

and drew a makeshift spreadsheet. "Let's start with our expense columns. Seeing what it will cost to run this business. We start on the left side with our initial investment, then continue downwards with our ongoing operational costs each month of $2000. Then add a column to the right for what our 'cumulative costs' are out of pocket. What you'd have to pay to run this short-term AirBnB."

He drew these on his napkin:

|  | EXPENSES | CUMULATIVE OUT OF POCKET |
|---|---|---|
| Initial | 7000 | 7000 |
| Month 2 | 2000 | 9000 |
| Month 3 | 2000 | 11000 |
| Month 4 | 2000 | 13000 |
| Month 5 | 2000 | 15000 |

"So," he said, "through 5 months, you've invested $15,000."

"Ouch," she said. "That seems rough."

He shook his head, "You're not thinking like a Dollar Farmer yet, Casey. Let's draw the 'income' columns."

Elijah stretched out his makeshift spreadsheet and added two columns: 'Income' and 'Cumulative Income':

| | EXPENSES | CUMULATIVE OUT OF POCKET | INCOME | CUMULATIVE INCOME |
|---|---|---|---|---|
| Initial | 7000 | 7000 | 0 | 0 |
| Month 2 | 2000 | 9000 | 4000 | 4000 |
| Month 3 | 2000 | 11000 | 4000 | 8000 |
| Month 4 | 2000 | 13000 | 4000 | 12000 |
| Month 5 | 2000 | 15000 | 4000 | 16000 |

Casey looked at the napkin and smiled as the reality of the math washed over her. "So you're saying that through 4 months, I would have spent $13,000. But I would have collected $12,000. And by the fifth month, I would have recouped my investment and started making money?"

Elijah smiled. "That's right," he said.

Casey took a deep breath. She said, "You know Elijah, not so long ago, the thought of doing something like this would have scared me to death. And it still kind of does. But what scares me more is the idea of spending the next 40 years of my life not being in charge of my own time. That failure is much worse than being too scared to try something like this out."

Elijah nodded, "It's an important lesson to understand: as humans, we gravitate away from pain and towards pleasure. We're wired that way. But pain is a far greater motivator than pleasure. So a person won't often make a fundamental change in their lives until the *'pain of staying in place is greater than the pain of change'*. I think, as it relates to being a Dollar Farmer instead of a Dollar Gatherer, you're in the midst of crossing that threshold."

Casey nodded in agreement.

"Now - I want us both to recognize that this example is an oversimplification," he said, "A perfect example of an *ideal* real estate Dollar Farm for someone who might have less than $10,000 in capital to start with. But - do you see how it's possible? How a person can stop trading hours for dollars and start creating their own revenue stream? Their own life?"

She sat back and smiled. "Anyone can do this. *I can do this.*"

Elijah smiled back. "So this is just one more way a prospective 'Real Estate' farmer can get started and make it."

Casey sat back as she pondered a thought. "What about real estate flipping? A real estate investor that buys a property, fixes it up, then sells it for a higher amount instead of renting it out. Is that a Dollar Farm?" she asked.

"What do you think?" Elijah countered.

"Hmm," she thought. "A real estate investor that buys a property then turns around and sells it for more isn't making a recurring, passive stream of income. They're making a one-time profit on a one-time transaction."

"Exactly," he said. "What do we call that?"

"That's 'hunting' - not 'farming'," she acknowledged. "Get paid once for a one-time sale."

"Correct," Elijah said. "*And there's nothing wrong with that.* Many people have made fortunes by flipping properties. But ultimately, that's not what we're talking about here. We're talking about *creating a stream of revenue that pays over and over for a singular effort rather than a singular payment for that singular effort.*"

"I get it," Casey nodded, "there's a big difference."

"Having said that," he added, "as a Dollar Farmer, it's smart to think about using your profits to reinvest in your next farm. Whether that's in the same type you're in or a new one."

"Like replanting your apple-seeds to start a new apple tree," she smiled.

"Exactly," he said. "At first, it will be attractive - and maybe necessary to hang onto your profits to keep food on your table. But ultimately, you can use the money you're making from one farm to start your next real estate farm."

She sat back, "Wow. I feel like I've learned a lot about real-estate investing in just a short conversation. Is there anything else?"

"There's plenty. We could talk about strategies that real-estate farmers use like 'BRRRR'," he said.

"Brrrr?" Casey laughed. "Is that a thing? It sounds like the makings of a winter storm!"

Elijah laughed too, "That it does. But 'BRRRR' is a real estate investment strategy that's very en-vogue right now. It stands for 'Buy, Rehab, Rent, Refinance, Repeat' to build out multiple real estate farms. It's one way to pursue other real estate rental ventures. There's other ways of owning real estate like through the use of Real Estate Investment Trusts - REITS for short. But I think those are conversations for another time. For now, I think we've covered enough in today's chat."

She asked, "Great. I loved what we learned about real estate. But I'm excited to learn about the next type of 'Capital' farm. I think we're up to 'business'."

"I agree. So let's first define our terms as we have in the past," he said. "When I say 'business' to you, what does that mean?"

"For me, it's what we'd said earlier about 'Commerce'. I think of a company that essentially sells a product or service," Casey answered. "That's what comes to mind when I think of 'business'."

"And for our purposes, that's not a bad start," he said.

Casey laughed, "I feel like I always have 'not bad starts' but that there's always more to it."

"I suppose in a sense, that's true! But I do want to commend you - it's best when we don't 'overthink' things. At its core, most businesses are simply designed as vehicles to sell products or services to customers," Elijah said. "But owning businesses is one of the oldest and most effective ways of being a Dollar Farmer. Like Real Estate, owning successful businesses is as old as time itself."

"I'll be honest with you, Elijah. The thought of owning a business is very intimidating to me. I wouldn't even know where to start," she said.

"I completely understand," Elijah agreed. "Buying and owning a business is scary. And a lot of hard work. And for what it's worth, you are already a business owner in a general sense."

"What do you mean?" she asked.

"Remember when you showed me your retirement account statement? In our first conversations?"

"You mean my 401(k)?"

"That's right. In it, you owned stocks and funds. Those represent small shares of ownership of different businesses. You own shares of those businesses which technically makes you a 'business owner'. Companies you and Jake shop at regularly like Amazon, Starbucks, and Walmart. Companies you use without even thinking about it like Apple, Google, and whatever car you drive," he said. "But while I'm a huge advocate for systematically building a stock portfolio, the reality is that it won't be a way for you to generate farmed income in a meaningful sense in the short run."

"So you'd still suggest I keep setting some money aside into a stock portfolio even though it won't help me generate much income right away?" she asked.

"Absolutely," he said. "It is still imperative that in the long run, you build 'outside' wealth by buying shares of ownership of good, quality companies by buying into the stock market. But it isn't the type of Dollar Farming we're talking about now. Which is why I want to have us consider the other types of 'business' ownership in the 'Capital' category."

"I'm all ears."

"You don't need to be all ears," he winked, "You're sitting in it."

She looked around and remembered the earlier part of the day's conversation. "A smoothie bar? You want me to buy this place?"

Elijah chuckled, "Not this place necessarily. But this *type of place* is exactly the kind that allows someone to become a business owner. And a business can be a very lucrative Dollar Farm if it is run well."

"Show me," she said.

"I want you to think of a business as an extension of what we'd talked about earlier: a 'machine'. In reality, a business that - like you said - exists to sell a product or service to customers does so by being a finely tuned system. Procedures and parts that work in a coordinated fashion to market, sell, and deliver its product to the paying customer."

She nodded, "Like a machine."

He continued, "Take this smoothie shop as an example: you knew to come here because you'd learned of it through its marketing efforts. Perhaps word-of-mouth or advertising. But somehow, it pulled you through the door. Once it did, it was designed to get you to purchase its product which has been crafted both at a factory and now here at the shop by machines and its friendly staff to serve it to you. You order, pay, sit down, enjoy it, and walk out the door. And if they've done well, you'll bring friends like me and tell others about it."

Elijah leaned in before continuing, "Of course, there are a

myriad of functions and processes to make all of this work. Finance and Accounting. Marketing. Sales. Machines and their maintenance. Custodial work. But do any of these functions *require* the owner's hands-on involvement?"

Casey sat back and thought about it, "I always assumed that business owners are very involved in their businesses."

"You're right," Elijah agreed, "many are. And many enjoy being very involved in their businesses - it brings them a sense of fulfillment. It's their baby. But - if the systems have been set up correctly and if the employees have been hired, trained, and managed correctly, does the business require the owner to be involved on a day-to-day basis?"

She smiled, "I guess not. I suppose an owner can let her business run and generate income if she's done it right."

"There's a philosophy that encourages a symbiosis for a successful business. It's made up of the '3 Ps': *Product, Process, and People*. If an owner can get those 3 right, they can have a business that will generate recurring revenue for them for life. Now - I want to emphasize that most businesses will require some involvement of their owners. It would be foolhardy to assume that a business doesn't need some involvement at the highest levels from time to time. But it is absolutely not necessary to 'live in' the business day after day."

Casey looked around, admiring the smoothie shop. She saw it through new eyes - not the eyes of a patron but through the eyes of an owner. She saw the brightly colored wallpaper and posters. The machines designed to mix and make smoothies. The menu board, carefully curated to entice customers to buy add-ons and upsize. And the upbeat teenagers working behind the counter, gleefully serving their customers. She could see how this business was a carefully crafted machine built with the right people, product, and process. A 'system' as Elijah had described it. And one - if it was well managed - that didn't need an owner involved every day.

"I can see what you mean," she said, "but I can't imagine starting a business from scratch without being totally immersed and involved - at least not for a decent period of time."

"You are absolutely correct," Elijah agreed. "For a 'startup' business, it is almost impossible for the owner to not be heavily involved in day-to-day operations for quite some time. For those types of businesses, my suggestion of the owner who aspires to financial freedom is that they build their business with an understanding that the sooner they perfect the '3 Ps' - their product, people, and process - the sooner they'll be able to step away. They have to think like 'Farmers' and not like 'Hunters and Gatherers'. But there are ways other than as startups for Dollar Farmers interested in being business owners to jump in and not be as actively involved from the 'get-go'," he assured. "Those are the ways we'll discuss now."

"I'm eager to hear," she said.

"So we agree - a 'startup business', one that is literally getting built from the ground up is going to require very active involvement from its owner - at least initially," Elijah taught, "But what kind of business wouldn't require that?"

"By the standards you just described, one that isn't a startup. One that isn't being built from the ground up," Casey answered.

"Right. And what types of businesses might fall under that umbrella?"

She thought about it, then said, "I guess an 'existing business'."

"Great - that's the first example," he said.

"But how does somebody who doesn't have a business suddenly have one that isn't a startup?" she asked.

He smiled, "By buying a business from someone who's already built it. In any given market in any given year, there are countless successful businesses where an owner who did the heavy lifting of starting and developing the system with the right people, product, and process, is looking to 'retire'. And the way they are hoping to accomplish that is *by selling their business*."

"So these are business owners who probably are very involved in a business that they built from scratch and did well over time," she pondered. "I'm guessing they 'lived' that business. And now, they want their financial freedom."

"But in their eyes, they can only get it by selling the business. Their relationship to their business is so entrenched, it's difficult for them to not see themselves 'in it' while they still own it," Elijah said. "So there's an opportunity for a Dollar Farmer to buy it."

"Still, the idea of buying someone else's business? That seems insane to me," she remarked.

"I understand. It'd be a scary proposition to buy a business," Elijah said. "But if you take a step back and consider that you're buying a 'system'. You're buying an existing farm."

"That's an interesting way to look at it," she said. "So if I'm a prospective buyer of a business as a 'farm' as you described it, I guess I'd want to be sure of a few things: that it has been planted and cultivated correctly. And that the people who are tending to the crops are the right ones for the job."

"That's exactly right," he said. "You'd need to do your due-diligence - just like an investor of a 'Real Estate Dollar Farm'. They wouldn't buy a rental property without checking the numbers and the math."

"The 'Return on Investment'," she agreed.

"Correct! So a prospective business buyer would need to understand the 3 Ps of that business: their people, product, and process. Are they sound? Are they working well together?" Elijah said.

"And I'd add a 4th 'P' to that equation," Casey observed, "their 'Profitability'."

Elijah sat back, beaming. "You are 100% correct and I'm so proud that you identified that most important consideration. Ultimately, the prospective farmer who is buying a business is *buying a revenue stream*. They are buying cash flow. And it better be positive. Profitability of that business is tantamount to whether it's a good investment or not."

She said, "So how does a prospective buyer find a business to buy? And how do they determine whether it's a good investment?"

"Finding a business to buy is the 'easy' part," he answered. "There are business brokers and 'business for sale' websites whose job it is to match prospective buyers and sellers with each other. Whether they're a good purchase? That's the hard part. It requires a person to dig into the details. And because every circumstance and every business is different...."

"...every evaluation will be different," she deduced. "I'm guessing that goes beyond the scope of this conversation."

"It does," Elijah agreed. "Except that I'd want you to know it's out there. They're out there. Businesses that are solid - profitable with good people, products, and processes. If it's the type of business that has a *Market* and aligns with your *Abilities* and *Passion* - if it fits your MAP, then it may be the right opportunity for you."

"But how do I get the money to buy a business? Obviously, these things aren't 'free'," she said.

"That's a great question," he acknowledged. "But hold your thought Casey because first, we should discuss another type of business a person can own that isn't a 'startup'," Elijah said. "Now I'm thinking of a different type of business - not one that I'm buying directly from a business owner but instead, one that

I'm buying into that has an existing 'system'. What kind of business opportunity exists for that so that a prospective farmer can buy in?"

She sat back, puzzled by his question. Casey dug deeply but couldn't find an answer.

"Look around, Casey. Where are we?" he asked.

She saw the smoothie bar around her and after a moment, it dawned on her. This wasn't just a Mom and Pop shop. This was a national brand. "A *franchise*," she smiled. "A prospective buyer can buy a franchise and own a 'system'. The products and the process. They just need to find the right 'people'."

"Exactly right, Casey," he said. "And there are very good franchises available in all types of businesses. Like smoothie shops and fast food restaurants or the yoga gym we went to earlier. There are franchises that specialize in providing care to seniors and others that are geared towards housekeeping. If you can think of a business, there's probably a franchise for it."

"But I'd always thought that franchising was expensive. And frankly, kind of a scam," she shared.

"Like any business opportunity, the franchise needs to be carefully evaluated. There are in fact awful franchises out there," Elijah agreed. "But good franchise opportunities also exist - ones that have developed the right set of products and processes that support their franchisees and help them towards success."

"So back to 'due-diligence'," Casey said.

"Without question. Perhaps more than any other category, 'Capital' Dollar Farms will require the most up front analysis because the prospective farmer is laying out something beyond their time that they might not get back," he said.

"Their money," she said, finishing his thought. "And where do prospective farmers get the money they'd need to buy a franchise or existing business?"

"Ah, that leads to the fourth and final type of farm we'll discuss in this category," he smiled. "When you and Jake bought your home, where did you get the money you needed to move in? The funds above and beyond your down payment?"

"We borrowed it," Casey answered. "We got a mortgage from our bank."

"Therein lies the first answer to your question," he said. "There are loans available to would-be Capital farmers that are geared specifically for new business owners and real estate investors. The Small Business Administration - the SBA - has loans, information, and resources for all types of funding."

"But you said this leads to the fourth type of farm in the 'Capital' category. What did you mean by that?"

Elijah said, "Because another way you can use your money to make money is to lend it. And in the same way that the bank gets paid interest from your mortgage payment, you'd earn interest as a lender."

"So I can be like a 'bank' for others?" she asked. "How would I do that?"

"You'd need a fair amount of capital to participate in a Farm like this and receive a meaningful income," he said, "but it can be a way to diversify your income streams and have your money pay you back."

"So after I have a successful farm or two and have been able to save some cash, put it to work by lending it out? You mean instead of leaving it in my savings account?" Casey pondered.

"Like I'd said earlier, I'd love you to invest in a stock portfolio. That's one way to build liquid capital. And of course, you always need money in your checking and savings to pay your regular bills. But if you think about it logically, you're already a lender. When you put your money in a savings account, you're 'lending' your money to the bank. They in turn, use your money as a reserve to lend it to others at a higher rate. Such as in a mortgage," he explained. "So the idea here is that instead of 'lending' the money to the bank at a low interest rate, you can get paid higher rates similar to a bank."

"But how would I do that?"

"As with most opportunities, there are resources available if you just go and look for them," Elijah said. "For example, 'Lending Tree', 'Lending Club', and 'Prosper' are platforms set up for regular people who have capital available to lend."

"Wow, I'm going to check that out!" she said. "I feel like we've covered so much. Is there anything else to discuss about the 'Capital' type of farm?"

Elijah smiled and slowly shook his head. "I think it's time to go to the next steps, Casey."

**EXERCISE |** Make a list of 'Capital Dollar Farms'. Consider what makes it a Dollar Farm, i.e., how it generates recurring revenue for its farmer. Consider what makes it 'Capital', i.e., what is the asset that is purchased by the Dollar Farmer that generates income on a recurring basis. Then, decide the degree to which this type of Dollar Farm resonates with you. Use the template located at www.TheDollarFarmer.com.

### Chapter 20

# Choosing Time

"So, what do I do now?" she asked.

"Remember earlier when we'd discussed the CASH process?" Elijah reminded her.

"Choose, Arrange, Sow, and Harvest," she recalled.

"It's 'Choosing' time, Casey," he said. "The first *Choice* of course, is to decide if in fact you will be a Dollar Farmer. Will you make the choice to stop trading your hours for dollars and instead, generate recurring, passive revenue?"

She nodded, "Yes. I made that decision long ago. I think of myself as a hard-working person who will always want to be productive in the world. But that doesn't mean that I have to give up autonomy over my time. I've chosen to be a Dollar Farmer."

"Very well," Elijah said, "Of course, I didn't think you were this engaged for this long in our conversations to not have made that choice. But at the end of the day, it is still a decision that you had to make of your own accord."

They smiled, knowing that they'd arrived at a moment of truth. He continued, "Then, the next 'Choice' is what type of

Farm you want to develop. We've explored each of the categories and taken a look inside. Now it's up to you to 'Choose' using the MAP method."

She sat back, a sense of excitement gurgling within.

*It's 'Choosing' time, she thought.*

**EXERCISE |** Look at the list of 'Creative', 'Commerce', and 'Capital' Farms you created from the previous exercises. Add any more that you've thought of to those respective lists. Now, categorize your own list using the M.A.P. process for yourself. From the list of farms, select those that resonate for you from the perspective of 'Passion', 'Ability', and 'Marketability'. Which of the farms excite you? Which are you most 'drawn to' or 'compelled by'? If you had to choose just one farm of the various options, which would you choose? Use the template at www. TheDollarFarmer.com to help you.

# PART IV

# "Harvest"

"Nature does not hurry,

yet everything is accomplished."

—Lao Tzu

## Chapter 21

# How Did We Get Here?

Nearly four months passed between Casey and Elijah's next meeting. They'd been in touch but they agreed that she and Jake needed to start taking these next steps on their own. The couple worked diligently through the MAP process. For 'Abilities', they identified their existing skills and talents along with areas where they'd want to cultivate new skills. They thought about things they enjoyed doing and felt engaged in for the 'Passions' column. And they brainstormed about the type of farm they'd want to be involved in with regards to 'Market'. After careful work and consideration, they made a 'Choice' and began the work of establishing three different farms.

Casey arrived back at the cafe on the farm where she and Elijah had first discussed the CASH process and opened the conversation to the different categories of Dollar Farms. He was waiting for her at the table with a glass of freshly squeezed orange juice.

"It's wonderful to see you, Casey," he smiled. "How are you?"

"I'm doing great. Thank you," she replied. She thought back to the first time they'd met at his golf club when she was in a state of despair over the idea of missing her father's cruise and how much it contrasted with her current, optimistic outlook.

"You seem great," he nodded.

She smiled, "I am so very grateful to you, Elijah. This process has been liberating. I have a completely new vision for my future. For my life," she expressed. "And none of that would have been possible without you and our talks."

"It has been my absolute pleasure and truly, most of the work has been yours," he said. "I'm merely here to help light a path for you. And as an aside, we're not done yet!"

"I know - there are still 2 more 'F's' to discuss!" she beamed.

"Yes there are," he agreed. "But first, I want to hear everything that you and Jake have done. Where are you on your farming journey?"

Casey smiled, "Well, the first thing you should know is that I've resigned my position at the company. I'm no longer a *Dollar Gatherer* at all."

"Wow!" Elijah exclaimed. "That happened far more quickly than I would have expected."

"My family cruise is next month," she said, "and I realized I'd never forgive myself - that I'd always have the regret of missing it if I didn't go. So I made a choice and pulled the plug. In our earlier lessons, when talking about 'Fulfillment', you'd said I'd need to find a '*Why*'. That it would help motivate me - especially when the heavy lifting of starting a Dollar Farm would tempt me back into Dollar Gathering."

Elijah listened intently as Casey shared her story.

"For me," she continued, "I had a very urgent, compelling initial '*Why*': to go on my family's cruise. To be there for my father." Tears started welling up in her eyes. "I *needed* to find a way to go. So I chose to become a Dollar Farmer."

He smiled compassionately. "That's inspiring. I'm so proud of you. You will never regret it. How's it going? What steps have you taken?"

"It's been quite an adjustment - especially at the very beginning," she shared. "But things are starting to fall further into place and it's becoming easier and more routine. We started by using the 'househacking' method you shared with us. We realized we have an entire room in our house that is essentially 'unused'. By renting it out, we were able to cover a meaningful part of our mortgage."

"Bravo!" he said.

"I don't think it'll be a long term solution because ultimately, we won't always want someone living in our home with us. But it's been a great way for us to get our feet wet and reduce our overhead in the short run," she explained. "Then we started looking at other types of farms - narrowing everything down with the MAP process. Using your wife as inspiration, I decided to start a few 'Commerce' farms based on my passion for yoga. I settled on a Print-On-Demand business selling logoed beverage tumblers and shirts along with a dropshipping business that sells yoga products, clothing, and accessories."

"Fantastic," Elijah said. "How did you decide on the different products and suppliers for your business?"

Casey smiled, "That's where the 'Arrange' part of the CASH process came in. We had to get organized so that we could have an effective and efficiently run business. For the dropshipping side, we did what you and I had discussed - set up a website by registering a domain and hiring a designer. We then added a 'Shopify' store and the 'Oberlo' app to search for products and suppliers on 'AliExpress'. There are literally thousands of available options - it can be overwhelming. There were a lot of late nights and big research projects. But once we'd decided on some, we ordered samples to be sure they met our standards. We did the same for our POD business."

"It is a lot of work just to get started," he commented. "Like we'd said, becoming a Dollar Farmer doesn't mean 'no work' or 'get rich quick'."

She nodded, "It was a lot of work. It still is. And there's been plenty of learning along the way. But what's interesting is that in a lot of ways, it never felt like 'work' - not in the traditional sense. It was never a 'chore'. I enjoyed all of it even though we weren't making any money yet. I felt like the brick-layer in your parable who was 'inspired' about his work because he could envision the future fruits of his labor - that he was building something meaningful to him. He had his 'why'. So for us, it never felt like 'work' - because I have my 'why'."

"That's great! So what's happened since?" he asked.

"So we jumped into the 'Sow' part of the business. We'd made our 'Choice' and finished 'Arranging'. It was time to put our learning and research to the test. We went public with our website," she said.

He sat back and smiled.

She continued, "We realized immediately that we needed to start driving traffic to the website and find ways to make sales," she said. "If it had been a different Dollar Farm, we might have made different choices. Choices geared around the needs of those farms. But for these Dollar Farms, we felt there were specific things that had to happen to bring our business to market."

"I'm so delighted you said that," Elijah acknowledged. "Each Dollar Farm will have its own set of considerations required to make it successful. What did you do for yours?"

"We did 3 things: I made 'how-to' videos that could be viewed on our new YouTube page but that would also embed within our website. Basic yoga instructional videos. Then, we launched ads on different Social Media sites like Facebook and Instagram targeted to yoga enthusiasts. And lastly, we have developed our own Social Media profiles for the business that post regularly."

"How's it going so far?"

"At first, there wasn't very much bang for our buck," she said. "It might have been very discouraging if I'd let it be. But really, I didn't expect there to be very much overnight success. A farmer doesn't plant an apple tree and expect fruit the next day."

"That's right," Elijah agreed, "It's a very different mindset you must adopt as a Dollar Farmer. You have to become *'comfortable with being uncomfortable'* - knowing that unlike Dollar Gathering where there'll be a regular paycheck starting week 1, it can be incredibly sporadic at first as a Dollar Farmer. Dollar Farming isn't for everyone."

"It did make it a lot easier that Jake continued working and that his paycheck along with the income from our tenant helped keep our 'Flow' positive," she said. "We have been careful to monitor our spending. And if it had been me handling this all by myself, I would have probably gone slower with regards to leaving my 'day job' while knowing I would have had to work harder as a Dollar Farmer at night."

Casey sat back and took a drink from her orange juice. She continued, "In the second month after the launch of our online store, we made a few sales so it was nice to see a bit of money trickle in. At least, it validated some of our efforts," she said. She sat back and smiled, "But this past month, things began to click. We got great reviews for the first products we'd delivered and that led to a bunch of repeat purchases and new orders. Success breeds on itself and by the end of this month, I'm projecting to already receive about half as much farmed income from my

POD and dropshipping farms as I had from my paycheck at my former employer."

Elijah sat back in stunned delight. "That's amazing, Casey. That is so much faster than even I could have anticipated. Do you have anything you attribute this to?"

She nodded, "We have been exceptionally careful to be sure that the quality of the products we deliver is top notch but at a price point that is fair. Our niche is 'premium products at everyday prices'. We realized as consumers that we'll support a business that sells us high quality products at prices we can afford. And that we'd be repeat customers. We figured that others would be the same."

"That's very astute of you - especially as you're just starting out. Like we'd discussed," he expanded, "your reputation can help you build this business and carry you forward. But if you damage your reputation and credibility by selling low quality products with high profit margins in hopes of making a quick buck, you'll find that you'll almost never be able to regain your reputation."

Casey nodded, "It's like the old adage: 'underpromise and over-deliver'. We set reasonable expectations that are easily exceeded when our customers receive their products. The most amazing part is that it's exactly like you said: we don't ever have to handle the products. Everything with regards to the manufacturing, shipping, and billing happens behind the scenes."

"Kudos," Elijah said. "And how's Jake feeling about it all?"

"He's very happy and very supportive," Casey smiled before turning away. "But I'm not sure if he's ready to 'pull the plug'. I'm not sure he wants to be a Dollar Farmer. And honestly," she said, "I'm not sure what to make of that."

"What do you mean?"

"I guess I'd thought that he'd be 'all in' on the idea of being a Dollar Farmer like me - that we'd have a shared vision so that we could manage our lives together this way," she answered. "But I'm not so sure about that anymore and I'm concerned as to how that might affect our future together."

"I completely understand," Elijah said. "This is a seismic shift in so many ways. It affects the way you earn income, the way you organize your time and life, not to mention the ways it requires a change to the mindset you've had your entire life. And ultimately, Dollar Farming isn't for everyone. Jake might be passionate about the work he's pursuing and it may be the wrong choice for him to leave his career path."

"He is absolutely passionate about his work," Casey agreed, "and I think that's what is driving him."

"But that doesn't necessarily mean that you two can't have a wonderful, fulfilling life together," Elijah said. "And you certainly don't need to make those kinds of judgments about your future this early in the process."

"You're right," she acknowledged. "I guess I'm just so excited about the possibility of having total freedom over my time that I'm surprised he didn't jump at it with the same enthusiasm as me."

"I understand," he nodded. "And, as you are often prone to do, created a great segue into our next conversation."

"It wasn't my intention," she laughed, "but I'm happy to hear about what's next!"

"Great," he smiled, "but let's first recap the first four 'F's we've explored to arrive at this point."

"We started our conversation with the first 'F', which was 'Fulfillment'. It helped frame our conversations towards the idea that our life and time should be our own but that we should also take heed at the fact that ultimately, the objective was for that life and time to be 'fulfilling'."

"Good - and I'd add to that the need to be mindful of being

productive, contributing members of society as an important ingredient of 'fulfillment'."

"That's right," she said. "Next, you taught me about 'Flow'. The idea is that it is impossible to live without 'money' - it is a necessity in our society. And that as a result, our existence will always have 'expenses'. To compensate for those expenses, we need to have 'income'. The relationship between income and expenses is known as 'cash flow', or for our purposes, 'flow'. Ultimately, we need to be aware that to be financially healthy - we must maintain positive cash flow," Casey concluded. "In other words, more income than expenses on a regular basis."

Elijah nodded in agreement as she continued, "As Dollar Gatherers and Hunters, our income flow would be described as 'earned' or 'active'. You have to actively work or 'earn' each dollar you are paid. Our objective as Dollar Farmers is to transition our income flow to be 'unearned' or 'passive'. Our work is leveraged by continuous income flow."

"Bravo," Elijah smiled.

"The next step was to understand the importance of building a 'Foundation'. Dollar Farming - like actual farming - doesn't yield results overnight. And early results can be sporadic and irregular," Casey surmised. "So before embarking on a 'full-time' effort to build a recurring revenue flow, a Dollar Farmer should make sure they have paid off any consumer debts like credit cards and built a 'reserve'."

"That's right," Elijah nodded, "And how much should a farmer save in their reserve fund?"

She smiled, "That's a trick question. There is no specific 'amount' since no two farmers will be in the same set of circumstances. There's an intuition a farmer needs to trust. But in general, it needs to be an amount that will allow a farmer to weather an extended period of time with little or no income - especially if they don't have any other sources of flow," she explained. "Jake and I were able to get away with maybe a little less of a reserve than most because he is still earning money from his work."

"And because you took advantage of 'house-hacking' right away," he added. "So what comes next?"

"Next is 'Farming'. There are 3 basic types of Dollar Farms: Capital Farms where you own assets that generate income, Creative Farms where your intellectual property becomes the product that a customer buys, and Commerce Farms where you actively sell goods using a repeatable process. To determine which farm - or farms you'd like to develop, you utilize the MAP process," Casey explained.

"And what's that?"

"It's determining whether a Dollar Farm addresses the 3 requirements it'd need to be successful and fulfilling: 1) It must have a 'Market', 2) the Farmer must have or gain the 'Abilities' required, and 3) the Farmer must have 'Passion', interest, or enthusiasm."

Elijah sat back and smiled as he commended Casey, "Well done. You have been a phenomenal student."

"Thank you, though there is still more to learn, it seems!" she said enthusiastically.

"I brought us back to this farm for an important reason, Casey," he smiled coyly.

"I can't wait to hear what's next," she smiled back.

Chapter 22

# The Trap

"Tell me a bit about all the things you ate today here at this farm cafe and how they arrived on your plate," he coaxed.

"Well," she thought about it, "I had a grilled chicken sandwich with vegetables and a side of sweet potato fries with homemade ketchup. So I imagine that a cook prepared it and the server brought it here."

"That's the short version," Elijah said. "But before the cook got his hands on it - what needed to happen to get this food on your plate?"

"Wow - a lot happened, I suppose," she remarked. "I guess a chicken had to be raised and slaughtered. Is this what you mean?"

Elijah nodded, "Yep - this is exactly what I mean. Continue."

"Vegetables and fruits were planted and harvested. Cheese was produced from one of the goats who also had to be taken care of. I'm not sure what else went into the meal but certainly, a lot of ingredients had to be grown and cultivated before they reached the cook's hands in the kitchen."

"That's right," he agreed. "And only then, did a team working in the kitchen prepare the food and bring it to our table. Not to mention all of the other things that go into running the cafe side of this farm. Dishwashers, laundry service, bookkeeping. The list goes on and on."

"I'm certain it's a lot of work," Casey remarked.

"And all this time, we've talked about how farming is a way to uncouple work from the harvest. That a farmer 'works once' and enjoys recurring harvests. And yet, clearly, there's work that needs to always get done," Elijah explained. "How do we reconcile that?"

"I never really believed that a farmer works 'only once'. I recognized that there'd always be work on the farm," she replied.

"Of course. But still - *this is a lot of work*," he responded. "Farming - and in this case, meal preparation - requires lots of work, doesn't it?"

Casey nodded in agreement. "And you always did say that this wasn't a 'no work' proposition or that it would be 'get-rich-quick'."

"That's true. But it was intended to remove some of the burden of work to give us back our greatest asset: time."

She looked on, knowing there was more to come.

"When we started," Elijah continued, "what was our objective?"

"To unlink 'work' from 'income'," she answered.

"Sort of," he said. "But that's really the tactic of what we wanted. The 'how' as opposed to the 'what'."

"I'm not sure I understand," Casey shook her head.

"When we first sat down and you told me you'd be missing your family's cruise - you realized something about your life and how the career trajectory you were on would affect it," he said.

"That's right. I remember thinking, *'my life is not my own'*," she acknowledged.

"And how did that make you feel?" Elijah asked.

"Like a prisoner," Casey answered.

"And what did you yearn for?"

"To be free."

He sat back and looked at her, waiting for the acknowledgement to come.

"Freedom," she smiled. "The 5th 'F' is 'Freedom'." She paused, reflecting on their conversations before continuing, "Financial Freedom and Fulfillment. It's what we've been discussing - everything has led to this...."

"Good," he whispered. "Now look at this farm and the cafe where we sit. Think of all the work that has gone into serving you this delicious meal you enjoy. If the farmer must by herself raise and slaughter the chickens. Milk the goats to make the cheese. Sow the seeds for the vegetables that will then be plucked. If the farmer must then cook and bring all of those items herself to our table - is she 'free'?"

Casey shook her head, "I suppose not. She's still a prisoner."

"That's right," Elijah said. "But do you imagine that there is a single farmer who is doing all of these things here by herself?"

"No way! It's not possible," Casey acknowledged. "There are different people, I'm sure, who do all of those things."

"Good. Now, I want you to go back and remember one of our earliest conversations," he said. "While you were a Dollar Gatherer at your old company - you were actually..."

"...farming for them," she finished. "I remember. You'd said that while I'm a 'Dollar Gatherer' for myself, I'm really 'farming' for my company." Casey paused. Then, "But I'm confused - I've been farming for dollars - for myself - not anyone else. I've started my own Dollar Farming journey. And I'm starting to feel 'free'. What's the distinction?"

"I'm glad you're asking. And I'm glad you're challenging

me," he answered. "It's because it's important that you recognize context, your role, the continuum, and *the trap*."

"The trap?"

He nodded.

"What do you mean?" Casey asked.

"You are doing a great job - I certainly don't mean to undermine your success. But from the minute we started, I said there were 6 'Fs' in this process and I'd said that for a reason: often, people mistake hunting and gathering for themselves as farming. And the result of that is never 'freedom'," Elijah said.

"I'm so confused," she laughed.

He laughed too, "Good! Because there's an important lesson here that I want to make sure we emphasize as you continue down your path." He took a sip of his orange juice and continued, "You are a 'Dollar Farmer' now, Casey. You are building streams of recurring income flow. But what that also means is that you are a business owner. And to truly be 'financially free', you have to think like one. Act like one. Be one."

She listened intently.

"The company you worked for - what was your role in that organization?"

"I was a marketing executive," Casey answered.

"Were you a Dollar Farmer in that role?" he asked.

She laughed, "Of course not! I was a Dollar Gatherer. We've already realized that."

He nodded, "Good." Elijah countered, "So was the business a 'Dollar Gathering' operation? Did the owners get paid based on the number of hours worked?"

She gave him a quizzical look before acknowledging, "No. I'm guessing our efforts helped the partners get paid more - or less - if we didn't do as well. But ultimately - the company was built to deliver profits which the owners received."

"That's right," Elijah agreed. "So if we turn our attention back to our meal today, someone was paid to plant the vegetables and harvest the vegetables just as you were paid to market your company's products."

"Agreed," Casey said, "but what you're saying is that while we were gathering dollars for ourselves, we were actually farming for someone else."

"That's right!" Elijah exclaimed, "You can see it now, right?"

"Yes," she nodded, "but it makes me feel as if I - and everyone that works for a business has been exploited."

"I understand how you feel," he affirmed. "And certainly, there are many people around the world who are being exploited. But free people in free societies have a choice of self-determination. And in our free societies, there are many who are quite comfortable and satisfied with dollar gathering for themselves while farming for others. They'll never aspire or be willing to take the risks of becoming Dollar Farmers. *And there's nothing wrong with that.*"

"Okay," she replied, "but I feel like there's a moral to the story here that we haven't quite come to."

"There is," he acknowledged. "I want to teach you about *the continuum and the trap*. Many people - very admirably - become frustrated with the idea of working long hard hours and careers for others. To feel as if their life is not their own - as you did. So they'll leave their position and 'start their own business'."

"That sounds like a good choice. A smart step," Casey said.

"It is," Elijah agreed, "except that many people mistake the idea of 'owning a business' with 'owning a job'."

"'Owning a job'?" she asked. "I'm not sure what you mean by that."

"Instead of being Dollar Gatherers or Hunters for someone

else's business, they become Dollar Hunters or Gatherers for themselves," he explained. "Imagine, for example, if Jake left his law firm to start his own practice - a very common and noble thing to do. He hangs a shingle and sets up his shop. Maybe hires an assistant or paralegal. Then, starts to look for business. How would he get paid?"

"I think right now he gets paid for billable hours," Casey replied.

"Bingo - and what happens if he doesn't have any hours to bill?"

She nodded, "He doesn't get paid. He's a Dollar Hunter."

"That's what I mean by saying, he doesn't own a business - he owns a job. If he stops working, revenue stops flowing. Whereas a true business doesn't require its owners or partners to continually do all the work," Elijah added. "And examples like this are commonplace across all kinds of businesses and industries."

"That's interesting. I don't think I would have ever considered that," Casey acknowledged.

"This is what I mean by *the continuum and the trap*," he said. "By continuum, I find the following to be the common path that many people who aspire to financial freedom take:

- Dollar Gatherers / Hunters who actually farm for others (the business they work for)
- Dollar Hunters / Gatherers for themselves (often, people stop here. *This is the trap*)
- Dollar Farm for themselves (this is the path you're embarking on)
- Have others Dollar Farm for you (true business ownership)"

"I think I understand," Casey replied. She took a pencil and wrote it on a napkin:

# Gathering and Hunting
## =
## Prison
# FARM FOR OTHERS
# HUNT FOR SELF

"It may be a bit dramatic to characterize it as 'prison' - especially those who go out on their own," Elijah observed.

"I know. But it's how I felt when I realized my days off would be dictated by the whims of my boss and company. And like we just discussed, many people who decide to leave their job and go out on their own to start their own business aren't actually becoming Dollar Farmers - they're just 'Hunting for themselves'."

"You're right. And often, they don't even realize it," Elijah said. "And that's the trap I want to make sure you avoid - even though you're already doing a great job."

"So how does one avoid falling into the trap?"

"Great question. First and foremost, you have to understand the nature of the business - make sure you are establishing whatever you do with a 'Farm' mentality. A recurring revenue model. If it won't pay recurring revenue, then it's not a farm," he started.

"But what about something like the example of a law firm like Jake's?" she asked.

"Good point. Let's take a step back and analyze his law firm's structure. Jake works for a firm where he is expected to produce billable hours. The firm itself likely has dozens of attorneys who all bill for their time. But the revenue flows up to the partners who have 'equity', that is, ownership of the firm. So while Jake is billing for his hours...."

"....he's farming for the partners," she said. "And if he started his own firm, to truly achieve 'financial freedom', he'd have to have other attorneys who farm for him."

Elijah nodded, "Yes - either that or create another revenue model that is not merely an extension of the 'trading hours for dollars' example. Beyond that, it will require the prospective Dollar Farmer to do two things to keep the work out of their hands: delegate and outsource."

"But aren't there some things that will always require work from the owner? Or the Dollar Farmer?" Casey asked. "For example, when we talk about an author as a Dollar Farmer, they'll still have to do the work of writing the book."

"Absolutely - there's almost always work that only the business owner can do and there is a likelihood that a Dollar Farmer will have to be involved in the tending of the Farm. The key for the Dollar Farmer is to be discerning in the work they'll accept for themselves as opposed to the work they'll delegate or outsource to others," Elijah explained. "A Dollar Farmer must continually ask herself: *Is this work that only I can do? Or could this be delegated to someone who could handle it instead?* If it can be delegated - at a reasonable cost - then it probably should be."

"That makes sense," she said. "An example would be the way I delegate the printing and shipping of the yoga products I'm selling with my new dropship business. If I had to manually do all of that, it would take up all of my time."

"Exactly," he remarked, "or as you said, an author must be responsible for writing the book. But things like 'cover art', 'editing', 'publishing' and 'printing' should all be left to others. Heck - even the writing these days might be delegated out. James Patterson, one of the best selling authors of all time actually has a team of ghostwriters who take his ideas and actually do much of the writing of the novels."

"Wow - I would have never thought of something like that!" she exclaimed. "Is this where AI comes into play? Tools like Artificial Intelligence?"

Elijah nodded, "Without question. Artificial Intelligence - AI as we might refer to it - is a tool that can absolutely support a Dollar Farm or business in ways that were unimaginable just a few years ago. For example, it is now possible to create a prompt for an AI tool like 'ChatGPT' to write a script for a YouTube video. Then, using an AI voice simulator to read the script and set it to the types of 'stock' videos you described when we were talking about 'filmmakers' with royalty-free background music. A person can publish a video that doesn't use their likeness or voice or even words that they've written and still convey a message that they'll get paid for every time someone watches it."

"I have to be honest," Casey said, "the world of Artificial Intelligence frightens me a bit. It almost doesn't seem fair. Like cheating."

"I understand why you feel that way," Elijah replied. "There are many ways that AI can be exploited to negative or even devastating effect. We're only just beginning to understand this new world we're in. But make no mistake - Artificial Intelligence is here and it is not going away. There is no putting this genie back in the bottle."

"So I better learn to understand it and embrace it where it can serve my needs," she said.

He nodded. "Automation is a reality. We're going to have to learn how to harness its potential responsibly."

She took a long look at the beautiful, lush scenery surrounding the cafe. She thought about the workers and farmhands who made all of it possible. And she realized that she understood to take this newest concept of 'Freedom' into account as she builds her Dollar Farms. She looked at Elijah and smiled, "Thank you. I think I understand the lesson."

He smiled back tenderly, "I know. Only one more before I consider you a 'Dollar Farm University' graduate."

## Chapter 23

# Forever

"These are beautiful," Casey remarked as she strolled through the art gallery with Elijah.

"Indeed they are," Elijah agreed. "Art is one of my many passions. One of my sources of fulfillment."

"This was the first place we met when I was still an intern working under my old boss," she said.

"Jordan Steele," Elijah smiled. "I remember how energetic and enthusiastic you were. But also clearly wise beyond your years."

She blushed and thought of herself back then - bright-eyed and excited about her role in the marketing department. How all of that would change after just a few years working in the company where she'd already started feeling like a cog in a very large impersonal machine. Now, under the tutelage of Elijah Bloom, she had regained herself and her freedom.

"Thank you for all you've done for me, Elijah. My life is on a completely different trajectory because of you," Casey said.

"Firstly, don't thank me. You've done all the hard work," he counseled. "And while it's true that your life might be on a different trajectory because of your entrance into Dollar Farming, it's actually a much, much bigger shift than that. The world - the course of history in fact, is on a different trajectory because of the change you've made."

Casey couldn't help but to laugh out loud, "What do you mean! Let's not overstate things! All I did was quit my marketing job and am now selling yoga stuff online!"

Elijah smiled lovingly, "I understand how it might not seem like much but I assure you - it is." He brought Casey over to one of the paintings and pointed, "Do you see this work? It was painted by a young, up-and-coming artist from the Amazon basin in Brazil."

"It's lovely. So inspired," she said.

"It will likely sell for $20,000 and the artist will donate most of his proceeds - after paying the gallery's commission to the indigenous tribe back in Brazil that raised him. Those funds will help preserve their land which has been devastated by the logging industry," Elijah said.

"Wow - that's super noble of him," Casey remarked.

"It's a labor of love - and something he's turning into a Dollar Farm through the sale of digital art, lithographs, and high quality reprints from his website," he said. "He's hoping to do his part to help fund and preserve the rainforest into perpetuity. Long after he's passed, his art and its impact will live on."

"Kind of makes me and my yoga business seem pathetic," she said.

"Not at all, Casey," Elijah said. "I merely use his example because it helps me easily illustrate my next - and final point: everything and everyone makes a difference. Everything you do, Casey, matters. It has significance. It's relevant. *You're relevant.*"

"I don't feel so relevant," she laughed.

"You might not feel it, but it's true. Every person who has

lived and every action they've taken has affected the destiny of the world. Even if in small, imperceptible ways, everything you do makes a difference through history for all," he explained.

"Oh come on, Elijah," Casey rebutted, "don't you think that's a bit of an exaggeration? *Everything* makes a difference?"

"*Everything,*" he affirmed. "The world is a different place by the mere fact that you are in it. And the choices you make are each like the ripple made when a stone is dropped into a pond. Some stones - and actions - make bigger ripples. But no matter how small, each ripple affects the current which in turn affects the movement and direction of each fish and plant within that pond and down its stream. Yes," he continued, "everything and everyone makes a difference."

"Hmm," she said as she gave him a critical look.

"One hundred years from now, the Amazon will be a different place because the artist made these contributions. And one hundred years from now, the world will also be a different place because Casey decided to leave her job as a marketer and become a Dollar Farmer," he said.

Elijah could tell that Casey was still skeptical about his premise. He proceeded, "Let's try a thought experiment: I want you to close your eyes, Casey."

She obliged.

"Now," he continued, "I want you to try and imagine a world in which you'd never existed."

"Whoa - that's heavy," she laughed.

"It is. But do it. Think of a world that never had Casey in it. Think of your parents. Would their life have been different?"

"Of course," she nodded - her eyes still closed.

"And what about your siblings? Would their lives have been different?"

Casey smirked, "They probably would have preferred it!"

"I'm sure you are a very good sister. But of course, their lives would have been different. And your family would have made different choices. Different choices about houses and schools and vacations - all because Casey wasn't in their lives," Elijah explained.

He continued, "And all of those different choices - and the different lives they had would have impacted the lives of the people around them. They would have met different people - interacted with others differently."

"Hmm," she reflected, "I never would have thought of it that way."

"And that doesn't even bring into the picture how you've impacted the lives of your friends - and your adversaries. The way you've affected your co-workers and clients or your community," Elijah said. "The world - and its history are and will be different simply because you existed. And now, it will be different because of the change you've made in becoming a Dollar Farmer."

She stared at Elijah quietly for a moment, reflecting on his comments. "Yes, I suppose so."

"And here's where you decide: how big of a difference do you want to make? There's no right or wrong answer - just something to reflect on. Because you are now taking ownership of your life and the choices you make with it will make a difference into perpetuity," he said.

"Into perpetuity," she smiled. Then, with a twinkle in her eye, she looked back at Elijah and said, "Forever."

He smiled back, "*Forever.*"

"That's the 6th 'F'. What we do and how we do it - the choices we make - make a difference 'Forever'," she expressed.

She looked around at the art that hung on the walls, recognizing that each piece would have an opportunity to live on long after the artist was no longer with us. And she understood the power of Elijah's words - that she too would make a difference but that the impact would be entirely dependent on the choices she made.

"Tell me Elijah, how did you know so much about the artist and what his mission is?" Casey asked.

He smiled, "I make it a point to know a lot about the artists we choose to represent in this gallery."

"Wait - this is your gallery?!"

He nodded, a slight blush filling his cheeks.

"This is one of your Dollar Farms?" Casey asked.

"In a manner of speaking, I suppose. Though it's really more my own labor of love - mine and Rebecca's, the gallery's curator. She is, after all, the art expert in the family," Elijah said. "But yes, we enjoy using the gallery as a way of promoting artists we feel strongly about while also exposing children to the fine arts - hoping to inspire a next generation."

"Is this how you got your start in Dollar Farming?"

He let out a hearty laugh, "Oh dear no! We'd have gone broke long before we'd ever have a chance to put food on our table!"

"So how did you get your start? As a Dollar Farmer?" she asked.

A sly grin swept across his face. "Do you remember the ATM at the gas station I sent you to? The one from your very first homework assignment?"

She nodded incredulously.

"That was my very first Dollar Farm. A single ATM machine that I purchased for a few thousand dollars. It made me those $90 I told you about that I told myself would pay my cable bill. The confidence of that purchase led me to buy another dozen machines. Eventually, I bought the gas station where that first ATM sits inside and built the car wash that goes with it," Elijah answered.

"So you're an ATM and Car Wash Dollar Farmer? Those are the businesses I sneered at during our talks!"

"I know! And you were onto something. Those Dollar Farms were - and remain - fantastic businesses. They generate great 'Flow'. But it was in the running of those businesses that I realized I was missing a vital piece - a piece that I since determined to integrate into every Dollar Farm I built."

Casey asked, "What piece is that?"

"The 'P' from our MAP. 'Passion'. It was then that I realized I wanted to build Dollar Farms that I was excited and enthusiastic about. And it's why I made it a point to share that with you," he said.

"So what did you do?"

"Well," he smiled sheepishly, "I bought a farm. An orange grove farm that was nearing bankruptcy."

Her jaw dropped. "You own the farm and cafe?!? I can't believe it!"

He laughed, "I saw so much goodness there but also an opportunity to create something marketable. So I took a chance."

"I thought it was a family-owned farm that goes back generations," she said.

"It is. It's my family's farm. One that was neglected and mis-managed. Nearly bankrupt. Now, it is profitable while also providing surplus food to underserved communities," Elijah explained.

"I'm in awe. So every place we went is a place you own?"

"Just about."

"The T-Shirt Factory?"

He smiled.

"The water turbine?"

"No - that's been there forever! But it's a place my Dad used to bring me. And I realized early on that it had a lesson whose profundity went far beyond the electricity it generated," he answered.

Casey sat back, admiring the art once more.

"Thank you again, Elijah," she said.

"And again, no need to thank me," he answered. "Go live your life - do good. Do good for yourself and for others. We need thoughtful people like you making a difference and using your time - your greatest asset - in ways that are meaningful and productive. Because your impact will last *forever*. But above all, enjoy your life. And remember *it is your life* - not anyone else's."

She nodded and gave Elijah a hug. Then, Casey smiled as she thought to herself:

"*My life is my own....*"

# Acknowledgements

This book is inspired by the memory of a person I never knew. My little brother, Miguel Angel was born prematurely on December 18th, 1974. 8 days later on Christmas Day, the nurse who would normally be entrusted to his care had the day off for the holiday and instead, a less experienced nurse was on duty. She tragically placed his feeding tube down the wrong pipe into his lungs effectively drowning him. He died soon after. I was only 2 years old at the time and never had the privilege of meeting him in person.

Over the course of my life, I've spent much time thinking about that incident and about Miguel Angel. I often wonder how my life would have been different had I had a little brother to grow up with. To play sports with. To talk about love interests. To race. Challenge. Wrestle. Lean on. Cry with. Hug.

My life would have undoubtedly been dramatically different as would that of the rest of my family. We would have known different people and touched them in different ways. Had my brother lived, our immediate circle would have had a different experience of the world which in turn would have changed the experiences of each of those people's immediate circles. It stands to reason then that there is a ripple effect we each make that carries far beyond ourselves. So by extension, the world is inarguably a different place than it would have been had my brother lived.

His young death and my ponderance of it have formed my own personal life philosophy: that everyone, no matter how small or seemingly insignificant, plays a role in the destiny of the world. We all matter. We all make a difference. You matter. *You make a difference.*

But this notion that we all make a difference by virtue of our mere existence is hard to reconcile when contrasted against Henry David Thoreau's quote, "The mass of men lead lives of quiet desperation". Do people sleepwalk through life with a simmering, subconscious angst pervading their spirit? Sadly, I believe to some extent many do. Maybe, as Thoreau suggested, most do. That to me, is a great tragedy. Does the ripple in history made by a life lived in "quiet desperation" regress and conversely, would a life lived with purpose and with intention make a greater, more positive impact? I believe it would. And this is largely the reason I wrote *The Dollar Farmer*.

Before it starts sounding as if I've gone off a transcendental deep end - particularly if you're thumbing through this book seeking answers to guide you to and through financial independence - don't worry: this book is squarely about achieving that end. You will gain the foundation and the method to achieving financial freedom. But the *raison d'être* - the "why" I wrote *The Dollar Farmer* is because ultimately, I am inspired by the idea that we can all make a difference. And by freeing our time through the liberation from work, we can pursue our greatest dreams, goals, and aspirations. And yes - we can also have lots more fun with the people whose company we enjoy.

In that regard, this book is inspired by and dedicated to the memory of the brother I never knew. So that we all have our best opportunity to make the greatest possible impact on the lives and causes that matter most to us. I hope this book helps you on your path towards that endeavor. And I hope it honors him despite the brevity of time he was on this earth.

But I would be remiss if I didn't also acknowledge the love and support of the people who counsel, encourage, embolden, and inspire me each and every day and without whom, this book could not have been written:

To my mother who taught me the wisdom and solace of love and compassion. Who taught me to always believe in myself. And who taught me to always, no matter what, pursue my dreams. Gracias Mami - le amo mucho.

To my father who never let me slide or accept standards that were beneath me. Who always encouraged me to not accept things at face value, to question authority, and to dig beyond conventional explanations in search of truth. To think for myself. I miss you Papi.

To my two sisters who - despite the challenges I threw at them and the torture I inflicted upon them when I was a young brother - always stood by me and have always had my back. And of course, thanks for all the PB&Js! I love you.

To my community of clients. Your support and patronage inspires me each day to work hard in service to your dreams and goals. I am ever grateful for you.

To Harry and Amir - thank you for serving as beacons of inspiration, for reading the manuscript, and for giving me your honest feedback.

To Tony and Sandra who believed in me from the beginning and without whom, my business would not have been what it is. Whose faith is resolute and whose love is transcendent.

To Louis and Genie who taught me the singularly most valuable lesson about being alive: "Don't Wait". May you both be enjoying that spectacular road trip in the hereafter.

To Tara, my office wife whose commitment to client service and willingness to do "all the little things" that keep our business running and our clients happy - all with a smile on your face - I appreciate you and your friendship beyond measure. Thank you. And yes - you can take Friday off.

To Safta whose grit, perseverance, and determination taught me to never, ever, ever quit. Am Yisrael Chai!

To Papa - who gave me the example of how to be a good husband and business owner. I will endeavor in your honor to always be strong and courageous.

To Jacob, my beloved son who challenges me, questions me, and forces me to try and be a better version of myself each and every day. Who, from the time you could talk, never yielded about being your awesome, unique, bad-ass self despite the harassment and bullying you endured. I love you son. Keep being you.

To Ariel, my dear daughter who works harder than anyone I know and who has endured more unwarranted hatred and attacks than anyone I know for merely spreading truth and love. And who, despite it all, remains a strong, loving, and a positive light in a dark world. I love you sweetheart.

And to my wife, my soulmate, my life partner, my best friend, and the most awesomest lady I know, Sharon. Thank you for literally everything. For encouraging me, for making me laugh and for being there when I cry. For keeping our household together when I worked too hard and for not doubting me when we didn't have two nickels to rub together. For enduring with me past the hard times and seeing what "could be" when there was nothing. This is for you. This is for us. And Sharon:

www.ingramcontent.com/pod-product-compliance
Lightning Source LLC
Chambersburg PA
CBHW021618120626
46545CB00001B/292